WHAT I BELIEVE

FRANÇOIS MAURIAC

WHAT I BELIEVE

Translated and with
an Introduction by
WALLACE FOWLIE

NEW YORK
FARRAR, STRAUS AND COMPANY

For my grandsons
Pierre Wiazemsky and Gérard Mauriac
when they are sixteen

Contents

❈ ❈ ❈

	Introduction	ix
I	THE STARTING POINT	1
II	EACH HUMAN BEING IS IRREPLACEABLE	15
III	MYSTERY ACCEPTED AND REFUSED	25
IV	THE DEMANDS OF PURITY	43
V	ENEMY BROTHERS	61
VI	TOM THUMB	83
VII	THE DEMON	93
VIII	THE DEBT TO PASCAL	101
IX	PRAYER FOR FAITH	115
X	REPENTANCE	133

François Mauriac

To the younger French reader today, M.
Mauriac is better known as a journalist, as an
academician, and even as a polemicist than as a
novelist. Even ten years ago, when he was awarded
the Nobel Prize for Literature, in 1952, Mauriac
was looked upon as a weekly adviser to the French,
as a chronicler and critic of social and political and
religious problems in his journalistic writings.

In the twenty-odd novels he has published—the
first appeared in 1909—he is the writer deeply
interested in the metaphysics of sin and drawn to
the secret unconfessed dramas of his characters. He
has been called too glibly a Catholic novelist, although in the strictest sense there is no such type
of writer as a Catholic novelist. A novel is not a

demonstration of a religious belief. It would be more accurate to say that François Mauriac is a Catholic and a novelist. In his essays, he is more a Catholic writer than he is a Catholic novelist in his novels.

The weekly articles that have been appearing for several years have been collected in book form from time to time under the titles of *Journal* or *Bloc-Notes*. In these pages he shows an aspect of his Parisian personality, an often embittered, vituperative and polemically minded Mauriac. He has demonstrated over and over again his greatness in daring to say everything he knows and believes about whatever controversial subject he is discussing. It is a permanent French tradition, illustrated today by a Mauriac as well as by a Sartre, that the writer must sustain the spiritual life of the country so that it will survive the horrors of party strife.

What I Believe is not in the least an unusual book for François Mauriac to publish at this point in his career. (The French edition appeared in 1962, when Mauriac was seventy-seven years old.) The early volumes of poetry, the long list of novels, and the plays had been interspersed with several volumes of religious essays. These books, written in the fervor of self-examination, composed in order to discern more clearly in the night of his faith the meaning of his religious life, have been contested far less than his novels. Such essays as *Souffrances et bonheur du chrétien*, *Dieu et mammon*, *Le jeudi saint*, analyze some of the major problems in the spirituality of our age. *What I Believe* belongs to this kind of writing and represents the quintessence of a work and of a life. It is a view looking back over a long life, a survey of a man's spiritual life. It is personal in the sense that Mauriac is primarily concerned with telling us how he has remained a Christian, although at every point in the analysis of his own spirituality he sees a relationship with the spiritual problems of his age.

At the very beginning he announces the tone and the quality of this discourse. He wants it to be direct and honest and naïvely simple. Since M. Mauriac is speaking of his faith, and since he knows that faith in its essence is simple, he is justified in this approach, which he sustains throughout the chapters. But the conflicts which arise from the holding of such a faith, the existence of nonbelievers, of strong spiritual forces in the world which are hostile to such a faith, add many difficulties of a philosophical and psychological nature which the writer does not avoid. He does avoid, however, a didactic approach to what turns out to be drama in a man's life. For Mauriac interprets his being born into Catholicism as a drama rather than as a chance occurrence. He narrates, with a feeling compounded of awe and humility, the vicissitudes of his faith—which he never lost—and its slow conquest of his life and the permanent victory it represents today for him.

His first communion, in May 1896, was followed by a very special kind of Catholic training in child-hood and adolescence. Women and priests dominated his early life. The piety of Mauriac's mother stressed all the ritual observances of religion, and instilled in her children an almost abnormal terror of carnal im-purity. When the young Mauriac began observing the provincial bourgeois society around him in Bor-deaux, he was struck by the discrepancies between the teaching of the Gospels and the behavior of the people in his social class. By the time he reached Paris as a young man, he was moving toward a liberal view of society. He refers to *Le Sillon*, a liberal Catholic organization, and describes how he was upset by its condemnation in Rome and by St. Pius X's encyclical *Pascendi* (1907), condemning aspects of modern thought already sympathetic to him. He realized that the literary and philosophical masters of his day, Maurice Barrès and Charles

Maurras, were not Catholic in any sense familiar or congenial to him. His childhood faith was not only a part of his life. It was an unattachable element of his sensibility, and it has guided him throughout his life in his search for the real meaning of justice and freedom and love. His faith has been his life. It has been the dominant force in his actions, in the achievements of his intelligence and in the impulses of his heart.

The chapter on purity in this small book raises questions which are central to the novels of M. Mauriac. He alludes to the problem of purity as he evokes moments of his childhood and certain moments of crisis when, as a young man, he wandered in a state of despair through the streets of Paris. In a very simple and direct way Mauriac tries to resolve this problem as he understands it. Sexual desire in man may become one of his chief glories, and it may become one of his chief catastrophes. Impurity is not, for Mauriac, in any sexual act as such, but rather in the spiritual deception and the lie with which a man is able to deceive himself.

It is clear from this treatise that Mauriac's faith imposed upon him a militant life in his social role as a Christian. He does not attempt here to expound a system or a doctrine, yet there is a thesis uniting all the chapters: the equation Mauriac wants to establish between faith and love. The thoughts which are expressed throughout the book on such subjects as love, freedom, purity and justice will doubtless be more acceptable to the majority of Mauriac's readers than the words expressing his faith in the manger once visited in Bethlehem by the Wise Men and in the empty tomb visited by the women on the first Easter Sunday. Mauriac is proud of this faith, and he does little to conceal it. But this pride is so instinctively joined with feeling and tenderness that one listens to his voice as that of a Frenchman, whom many look upon as the foremost writer today, impatient to testify to the truth as he understands it.

It is perhaps clearer in this recent book than in the others that the theology of Mauriac is very basic, even elementary. He is insensitive to the hope of modern man of matching his intelligence with the cosmos and conquering it. The sole conquest which holds him is that of individual salvation. His religious faith as well as his political commitments are related to this personal drama of each soul. He has been an indifferent parishioner, unattached to the group as a whole. He has even been impatient with the elaborate exterior structure of the Church.

And yet the ending of the book is one of peaceful submission to the Church in all its aspects; an almost childlike acceptance concludes Mauriac's meditations. His voice may well be the last of two generations of Catholic writers in France whose work has centered about a religious trust and inheritance. Claudel and Péguy were the giants of the first generation. The second generation, writers born in the eighties, includes Jacques Maritain (1882), Charles Du Bos (1882), Mauriac (1885), Georges Bernanos (1888) and Gabriel Marcel (1889). By his novels and his extensive critical writing, Mauriac has probably reached the widest audience of all of his contemporaries.

In his *Journal*, Mauriac writes that "a single novel is proposed to the Christian, his own; a single debate taking place between him and his Creator." His novels are problems posed by his faith. There is still much to be studied in Mauriac's metaphysical turn of mind which is completely instinctive, preoccupied with a very dark, very carnal vision of truth, one which grants little power to man's intelligence and man's will. As a novelist, he is always drawn toward the most secret and most blameworthy parts of his creatures' minds. His characters do not incarnate an ethical system. We see them living in a very particular atmosphere which may well be Mauriac's major literary creation. The summer heat in the section of France around Bordeaux, the sudden storms, fires in the pine forests, bird hunts, obsessions with the land and money—these are the elements of most of his novels.

In *What I Believe*, more than in most of his books, believers and nonbelievers will find a common ground. Believers will read in it a discussion of many of the theological problems which are theirs. Nonbelievers will recognize familiar problems and will be encouraged to read Mauriac's view of them, because of the pervading tone of dialogue throughout the work. The great Christian writers before Mauriac who have written on the problems of faith in the same mode of question and answer are Saint Augustine, Pascal, Kierkegaard and Dostoievsky.

Mauriac's position is unequivocably stated. He believes that Christ is God and that the Church is the guardian of the words of Christ. He believes in the words used by a priest when he forgives sins and when he changes the bread and the wine into the body and the blood of Christ. This faith, defined in these very few articles of belief, has never been shaken, not even when as a student he was deeply disappointed by the encyclical *Pascendi*. Mauriac is

the liberal in Catholic circles, and his humanism is
rooted in a Christology which he himself defines as
Pascalian. God is felt in man's impulses to charity.

Mauriac's personal drama, which he does not
conceal on these pages, is the contradiction he feels
between his successful career of a writer—during
which he has received honors and glory and lived
largely in terms of the pleasures of art and the in-
tellect—and Christian faith which is, according to
the words of Christ, a religion of poverty and
charity.

In his combativeness—Mauriac refers several
times to this trait in his character—he has inter-
preted literally what Catholicism has taught him
concerning the great human problems of equality
and freedom. In the major and minor causes of his
time, Mauriac in his public role of spokesman has
always defended the side of justice. He has kept his
eyes on the decisive world problems, and considered
them from a temporal viewpoint and from the viewpoint of eternity. The communications he has tire-
lessly made, of which this small book may be one
of the last, have always come from the noblest part
of his consciousness and from the loftiest part of his
nation's consciousness. Whenever, within these
communications, the religious role of his conscious-

ness has been emphasized, his writing has inevitably taken on greater depth. This book does honor first to Mauriac himself, in the vibrant insistency with which he speaks, and it does honor also to those for whom the book was written.

WALLACE FOWLIE

June 1963

WHAT I BELIEVE

This book is not intended for scholars or philosophers or theologians. I hoped in the most simple and direct way possible to answer the question, "Why have you remained faithful to the religion into which you were born?" This was almost like playing into the hands of the enemy. The risk is proportionate to the simplicity and ingenuousness that have kept me prayerful throughout my life, but that, from childhood to old age, have allowed me to feel and touch and possess a love I did not see.

I

❁ ❁ ❁

The starting point

* * *

WHAT I BELIEVE is not identical with what I know. This is the first misunderstanding that has to be broken down. So often people have claimed they envied me: "How lucky you are to believe you are immortal!" As if faith could be reduced to the possession of a certainty founded on evidence. Faith is a virtue—one of the three virtues called theological, and the first of the three. . . . By virtue is also meant use of the will, a meritorious and difficult use.

Initially I did not wish to believe, since I was born into a certain religion that I saw practiced around me as soon as I was able to observe and understand, and since I was told it was the most important thing for me to understand, and since—at the age when doubt is unknown and when our parents and teachers appear to us as the depositaries of all truth—I learned to venerate and love that religion less for itself than for the means it put within my reach and which established my relationship with God.

Notwithstanding this, my will had to intervene quite early, as soon as I felt my faith threatened and the first doubts. It was a will proportionate to the attraction I felt for everything that touched religion, and which was related to the senses, but also in proportion to the help I received from it, to the efficacy of prayer and a life of the sacraments which secretly enriched my temporal life.

In my adolescence I examined all the objections which belief in the supernatural proposes to a mind of average intelligence and especially, since it was the age of modernism and I was reading the works of Abbé Loisy, all the objections raised by historical criticism. But I confess that I always approached those objections with prejudice, with a desire to overcome them. My choice was determined in advance, and it was less the choice of a certain religion, of a certain Church, than of Someone with whom I communicated thanks to that Church and that religion.

Truly I cannot say that I love the Catholic

Church for herself. If I did not believe that she has
received the words of eternal life, I would have no
admiration for her organization and methods, and
I would loathe many chapters of her history. In
particular, I find the Albigensian crusade intoler-
able. I have always believed that I must have among
my ancestors (some of whom came from the prov-
ince of Ariège) a few who were burned alive. On
this point I am the exact opposite of a positivist of
the *Action Française,* who does not believe that the
Church teaches truth but who admires her as an
institution. So far as I am concerned, the Church—
and partly through her very defects—has kept intact the sacred trust she received. The fact that she
has codified, catalogued and defined this trust more
than we might wish is not important to me. What
does matter is that thanks to her, a certain Word
has come down to us, not as a memory, not as something that can be called to mind, but as something
active and living: "Your sins are forgiven you."
"This is my body given for you." The old canaliza-
tions did not affect me, nor the fact that they were
partly obstructed, from the moment that those two
Words flowed through them. The Lord warned us
about them in the prophecy of Isaias: "Once fallen
from the sky, does rain or snow return to it? Nay,

it refreshes the earth, soaking into it and making it fruitful, to provide the sower with fresh seed, the hungry mouths with bread. So it is with the words by these lips of mine once uttered; it will not come back, an empty echo, the way it went; all my will it carries out, speeds on its errand."

I am no longer troubled by any of the criticism leveled at the human organization of the Church. The worst of what I discover there in the past or of what I observe today still leaves me indifferent because the Church constitutes for me the entirety of the human means used by Grace to fecundate each of the souls who have recourse to that source of living water impounded in Rome.

It will be said to me that I am considering the problem resolved and that I should first answer the question, "What did you believe at the beginning, before accepting one particular religion? How was the act of faith born in you and how did it manifest itself?"

I am incapable of believing that life has no direction or purpose, that man has no destiny, as I am incapable of objecting to the testimonial of a thought, of a word, of a human countenance in themselves, and still more perhaps in their expression in art. Art would be for me the unchallengeable

testimonial of a God who is Love if there were **not**
that other witness within me, my conscience **who**
judges me and whom I question and who answers
me and to whom my most secret thought is answer-
able. This may seem rather pitiful to the philosopher. I am trying not to dazzle my readers with
flattering reasons but to give them the real reasons
of my faith. And those I have just said are indeed
the reasons which at the beginning were sufficient
to counterbalance the impossibilities that God exists, which had also occurred to me, because I was
not insensitive, even in my earliest years, to those
aspects of creation which appear bewildering and
unacceptable to our intelligence.

> *As if tired of His pure creation,*
> *God Himself broke the obstacle*
> *Of His perfect eternity.*
> *He became the One who dissolves*
> *His principle into a consequence*
> *And His unity into stars.*
> *The Heavens, His error! Time, His ruin!*
> *And the animal abyss, gaping*
>
> . . . . . .

It could not be said better. But man is here, and
I am here, and nothing can change this. The *no*

I oppose to the creation I am not free to oppose to
the fact that I exist, that I think, that I love and
that I do evil. So I affirm, with this negation, that
at one moment of time, on the surface of matter,
was discovered the germ which bore in itself this
endless passion. The more I think of it, the more
I believe that Christ appeared to me as the One who
decides between two impossibilities. It is He who
turned the scales, or rather—since the scales have
always been turned on the side of God since I have
been conscious of myself—it was He who kept me
from rejecting what my ancestors and education
had decided I would be: a Christian in the Catholic communion.

It was Christ alone, and not the beauty of Christianity and not the spell of the liturgy. Of course,
I have loved the house of the Lord and the place
where His glory dwells. But I can judge all this
better today: I took the same pleasure in "the stately
order of those ceremonies" as I did in all the mys-
terious elements of my childhood. The Church, with
its spectacle and its music, orchestrated the mystery
of childhood. My love for religion's appeal to the
senses and for its ceremonial was mingled with the
love of the child I was, a love I have kept alive in
me and whose presence gratifies my old age.

And yet I was the type of man, if I had not been a Christian, the least capable of coming to religion along the way taken by Huysmans. Certainly the liturgy would not have been sufficient (I do not even say to convince me) to attract me and hold me. The closer I live to God, the more intimate my sacramental life becomes, and the less need I feel for ceremonies. A Low Mass overwhelms me, and I no longer go very often to hear, as I used to once, the High Mass sung each day at ten in the chapel on the rue de la Source.

In Rome I am neither shocked nor scandalized by the pomp of the Vatican. But neither am I dazzled or really enchanted. I am grateful to the institution for what it has saved and protected and maintained. I give thanks to that old illustrious vessel for not being porous. But it is not for its beauty that I love it. Its beauty would not have convinced me to return to it if I had moved away from it.

I do not wish to write anything here that would cause anyone to doubt my feelings about the Church. The ambiguity comes from what we all imply by this word. For most men and even for most Christians, the Church denotes a hierarchy, an administration, an organization: a method for surveillance and control rather than a spirit. There is nothing in this that shocks and scandalizes me. In this regard, the Church is what channels the spirit and checks it when that seems necessary and which even stops the current. The temporal history of the Church, its relationship with Caesar and its insertion into this world for which the Lord refused to pray, does not entirely cover another very hidden story: that of the soul of the Church, manifested for me no better in Saint Peter's at Rome than in the poorest village church where the small lamp burns and which I prefer. For Saint Peter's in Rome was built with money from indulgences which cost the Church half of the people who joined the Reformation. This was putting architecture at too high a price.

But once again, I repeat what I believe: this organization safeguarded everything. Nothing was lost in the Catholic Church of the words which are spirit and life. For me, this comes from experience. I test and verify that these words coming down to me in and through the Church are spiritual life. It is true, I did not have to choose this body of Judaic-Christian beliefs into which I was born and which I was taught. But, as Pascal says, it is precisely because I was born into them that I was fortified against them. And although I was born in them, I have never ceased finding them different from all others; and especially, in practicing them from childhood on, I have not ceased feeling their efficaciousness.

No one could have less than I do the reformer's instinct, in spite of everything which in the visible Church shocks and irritates and scandalizes me. But the worst evil would be to increase the tears in the seamless tunic. There is nothing else to do save to join all those who are trying to sew it again into one piece. I have never worried about examining the trial of Rome and unraveling the reasons and excuses for heresies and schisms. I would not give up for anything in the world the sacramental life dispensed to me by the Roman Church, which in truth is for me the source of life and whose historical justification I find in texts, and in the oldest, the epistles of Saint Paul.

"The sins will be forgiven those whom you pardon. . . ." It is strange to think that what is a stumbling block for so many men—the confession said into the ear of a priest, the avowal of the worst of our acts to another man—corresponds precisely to the demands of my nature: my feeling of guilt, my need to be pardoned, the belief—the most unbelievable of all beliefs—that one word which has been transmitted for almost two thousand years suffices to remit sins, from the slightest offenses to the greatest crimes. A man who believes himself a sinner, who feels himself sinful, is already at the gates of the Kingdom of Heaven. This is what makes the difference between periods of faith and other periods. Men were not less criminal than they are today, but they recognized themselves as criminals. They belonged to what had been lost and to what the Son of Man had come to look for and to save. Today what is lost does not know it is lost.

This need of being pardoned, which has always been in me, which was the most widespread element in the world during periods of faith, is the rarest element today. For the death of God is at the same time the death of the consciousness in us of His will and of what it demands of us. I feel I am a Christian by the guilt separating me from God and by the faith in the means which the Church puts at my disposal in order to begin all over again, no matter what I have done, to begin with a clean page.

Like all human sentiments, this one offers a mediocre or even an almost despicable aspect, but also an aspect of nobility and holiness. What invites scorn is that search for spiritual comfort so developed in mediocre souls who believe themselves holy because they are scrupulous. But what is worthy of respect, in the sentiment I am describing, is the demands of our love, which knows by experience that sin separates it from the One it loves. Certainly the almost physical relief felt by the believer after absolution appears in the comfort I denounced and at which I blush. But it allows a joy that comes from grace rediscovered. And I can see why an agnostic would believe it to be an infantile reaction, because it is true that we react as when our mother opened her arms to us and when we were that sobbing child about whom they said "He repents easily. . . ." And that, certainly, I must admit and do admit. We must give our consent to the word of the Lord: "Unless you are like one of these little children. . . ." Well, yes, it is true. The Christian continues to obey, or rather begins over again to obey those impulses of childhood, but without shame, because he discerns in childhood not a lack, not an absence of attainment, but a spirit, a grace, a power to understand what is from God, to know Him with a knowledge quite different from that of philosophers and scholars.

At this point I imagine someone interrupting me: "What you believe comes to, in a word, what you feel, what you experience: the efficacy of the sacramental life which is uncontrollable and unverifiable for anyone else. And are you yourself sure of not being the chief contributor to the comedy? And what if the mystics were ventriloquists tricked by their own game who pretended to believe or who succeeded in really believing in the secret words they themselves uttered and which they ascribed to God? This would substantiate the belief that the sacraments affect only those who are inclined to use them, but not those who receive them passively without entering into the game."

II

❀ ❀ ❀

Each human being is irreplaceable

※ ※ ※

I INSIST I am not trying to minimize the role of the will in the act of faith. I have never concealed from myself my desire for God, my need for God which, more than fear, would be able to bring forth God. I have always been so persuaded concerning this (and how wouldn't I have been, knowing myself?) that I have always been on my guard. I would not have yielded to the inner call unless something from outside had answered. But something did take place in history. There is no point in saying that the reality of Christ can be called a "myth." This does not constitute an answer.

My faith is based upon a fact which, for so many other people, has been a stumbling block. Historical criticism, to which I have not been indifferent and which, practiced on my level, passionately, has not destroyed for me its subject, has brought closer to me the Gospel text and the Epistles. The more sensitive I was to certain suggestions and conjectures of Renan, Strauss and Loisy, the more vehemently I reacted to them. There has always been in me, even in the most troubled hours and in the greatest darkness, an attachment, an affection—I must say it since it is true—a love for everything that is witnessed to in all the verses of Scripture. And this passion, because it is a passion, transcended all rational certainty.

Where do this love and this grace come from? And why haven't all received it? But what do we know about this? What do we know about the grace bestowed on each one under many disguises, which has been refused or accepted in a proportion God alone knows?

The personal adventure, the individual salvation, the story taking place between each one of countless human beings and the infinite Being, which has caused so many doubts and raised so much mockery among the Scribes of so many periods, this impossibility, this absurdity has paradoxically become one of my reasons for belief and perhaps one of the most efficacious. In one of the novels of *L'Histoire Con-*

temporaine of Anatole France, M. Bergeret makes fun of some woman in the town who wants very much to be immortal and who believes she is. My colleague Jules Romains is also greatly amused by the fact that his concierge hopes never to die. The way in which a human creature, since a thinking man first raised his eyes to Heaven, was in communication with the unknown God, repeated in countless personal stories each one of which involves the infinite, is an unthinkable madness, but reaches a point which I wish I could encompass within myself, where it becomes the generator of certainty and hope.

A miracle we no longer even see, so commonplace it has become, is that no human face, despite the numbers that exist and have existed, reproduces another human face. In contradiction to the familiar simile, no one drop of water has ever been exactly like another drop of water. Among all the Negroes, among all the countless members of the Oriental races who may seem to be the same for us, there is not a single one whom his mother or his brothers or his friends would not recognize and would not distinguish from thousands and millions of others. There are not two faces alike in nature. There is not a single living being who reproduces exactly feature for feature one of the billions of faces that preceded us. A human being is a unique copy and has never been reproduced since the world has been the world. This singular irreplaceable characteristic of the humblest human creature, that is a fact and an evidence, that prevents our confusing any two persons and allows us to recognize them in the midst of a crowd—even those of the past, even if their features have been photographed very seldom (I would recognize Pascal or Rimbaud if they came into this room)—this singular characteristic helps me to understand that each one can be the hero of the drama of salvation whose stake is eternity. What helps me to believe that the Almighty participates in this with each particle of that dust of creatures which rises up and falls back on the surface of a planet, itself a particle of dust in the cosmos; what even makes my belief easy and habitual is the practice of communion, the Holy Eucharist.

Each of the communicants throughout the world partakes of the body of Christ. Each receives Christ. Each of the countless faithful at the Easter Mass where I was present this morning returned to his seat, his eyes closed, his hands clasped, God overflowing in him, each one alone with his Creator, and He was everything for everyone. This throughout the world on the day and the night of Easter: Christ truly living in each living soul. For the Almighty, it is in an eternal present that these myriads and myriads of souls until the end of time are here suspended and as if condensed around this small piece of living bread.

It is indeed strange that the Eucharist, which constitutes in the Christian mystery that which defies reason the most, helps me to believe, simplifies for me faith in that God who is reduced to the proportions of the most insignificant man and the poorest woman, to the degree of giving Himself to them as food if they want Him. My mind is such that I feel a deep satisfaction in this unbelievable humbling of the Almighty, in this absorption of the Creator by the creature. How many times since the twelfth of May 1896, when I made a good first communion, have I repeated and marveled at the words of Gounod's hymn sung on that morning: "Even to me You can descend, humility of my Savior!" (*Jusqu'à moi vous pouvez descendre, humilité de mon Sauveur!*)

Nothing is less natural to me than the impulse which encouraged Father Teilhard de Chardin to enlarge Christ to the dimensions of the cosmos. Not that I am shocked by this, because the priest therewith answered a need of our world today and he has greatly helped in the preservation of the faith in our atomic age. But I belong to another race of mankind. In my eyes, the deepest mystery is that of the Creator reduced to the dimension of each creature in particular, the least of whom, because he has intelligence and is suffering, is infinitely more important than the cosmos, which is blind and deaf and without conscience. I do not see what the knowledge gained by these last generations would add to what Pascal said concerning the two infinities. All of Teilhard de Chardin is, if not refuted in advance—but there is no reason to refute him—restored to the proportions of a personal viewpoint in the famous passage from Pascal. We do not fear quoting it once again since no truth more central, more influential, has anywhere been expressed in fewer words and with such precision, so well articulated and presented than this *pensée* of Pascal which seems to me the point of perfection in French thought and French writing. It is the extreme point both of depth and clarity. The least subtle mind can participate in this reasoning which contains the key to everything:

All material bodies, the firmament, the stars, the earth and its satellites are not worth the humblest human being. For he knows all that and he knows himself. And the material bodies know nothing.

All material bodies together and all human spirits together and all that they reproduce are not worth the smallest impulse of charity, which is of an infinitely higher order.

From all material bodies together, we cannot bring forth one single thought. That is impossible and of another order. From all bodies and human spirits, we cannot bring forth an impulse of true charity. That is impossible and of a supernatural order.

I am enlightened by this passage, and fully enlightened. Christian that I am, I do not believe myself condemned to the darkness more than any other man, although Christians are looked upon as adjusting to mysteries which confound man's reason. In this connection, what is my real thought?

III

✿ ✿ ✿

Mystery accepted and refused

✿ ✿ ✿

AT TIMES I try to imagine what goes through the
mind of a young Russian boy, if he remembers the
church where his grandmother took him secretly
when he was small. When he grew up, he perhaps
returned there out of curiosity and looked at the
candles burning in the semidarkness, breathed in
the aromatic smells, listened to the chanting of the
Psalms in the spirit of an ethnologist attentive to the
incantations of a black sorcerer and the sacred tribal
dances. I wonder what pity or what scorn those
mumbled prayers and incantatory gestures aroused
in him! Are there still benighted people who do not
know that there is no such thing as a mystery? I
have often said to myself that if this imaginary
Marxist boy questioned me about the best definition

to give to this surviving animal of a species he believes on the brink of disappearing and who is called a Christian, I would answer that the Christian is essentially a man who refuses all mystery, who does not allow the mystery a materialist has accepted and does more than accept—considers reserved and forbidden to scholars and philosophers. "Who are we? Where do we come from? Where are we going?" These three questions, which Gauguin wrote at the bottom of a famous triptych, are looked upon by the Christian as demanding an answer, and as being today all the more imperative since technology proves the almost-divine power which has been given us.

I have never been resigned to this mystery. I have not acknowledged it. I have never admitted the absurdity that uncreated matter could bring forth life, that the original germ could contain potentially the conqueror of space and galaxies. I must once again repeat what I have known since I read Pascal in my next-to-last year at the *lycée*: "The slightest movement of charity is of an infinitely higher order." I do not have to refer to the question asked by the face cut in marble and in stone in Athens or in Chartres, which looks at us from centuries ago, or by the complaint which constantly rises up and which we still hear, although it was Mozart's, who was thrown into the common grave so many years ago. I am not resigned not to look for an answer to the question raised by the thought which conceives, by the hand which shapes and especially by the heart which loves and suffers and which makes a man different, although he is similar, from millions of other men and women who cover the earth, each one as irreplaceable as he is himself.

I clearly received this answer, but it was contained within a mystery which needs no other answer save faith and love: the mystery of the Incarnation. In this way, I will at the end have accepted the mystery, but I began with the refusal with which I first confronted it. Agnostics and atheists, however, consent to it from the start, and do more than consent, for in their eyes the fact alone of asking this question relating to our origin and our end seems like an intellectual regression.

Faith, hope and love were born for me at that point where the refusal of a mystery met with the consent to mystery. I discovered the justification for the refusal I made in the light which had come into the world. To my knowledge there is only one character in the New Testament who is not a saint or a criminal or blind or enlightened. He is the only one about whom we can say that he is ridiculous. His name has even become a joke. And yet it was to that character, to that teacher, because he was a doctor in Israel and his name was Nicodemus, that the essential message concerning the two mysteries was spoken: the one I refuse and the one I consent to with all my heart and mind and whose name is *light*. This Nicodemus I must have resembled when I was a questioning child, because I was told over and over again: "What a Nicodemus you are!" This Nicodemus, this simpleton, this doctor in Israel heard nevertheless, concerning the Mystery, that answer which allows none other.

There was a man called Nicodemus, a Pharisee, and one of the rulers of the Jews, who came to see Jesus by night, "Master," he said to him, "we know that thou hast come from God to teach us; no one, unless God were with him, could do the miracles which thou doest." Jesus answered him, "Believe me when I tell thee this; a man cannot see the kingdom of God without being born anew." "Why," Nicodemus asked him, "how is it possible that a man should be born when he is already old? Can he enter a second time into his mother's womb, and so come to birth?" Jesus answered, "Believe me, no man can enter into the kingdom of God unless birth comes to him from water, and from the Holy Spirit. What is born by natural birth is a thing of nature, what is born by spiritual birth is a thing of spirit. Do not be surprised, then, at my telling thee, You must be born anew. The wind breathes where it will, and thou canst hear the sound of it, but knowest nothing of the way it came or the way it goes; so it is, when a man is born by the breath of the Spirit."

Nicodemus answered him, "How can such things come to be?" "What," answered Jesus, "can such things be strange to thee, who art one of the teachers of Israel? Believe me, we speak of what is known to us, and testify to what our own eyes have seen, and still you will not accept our testimony. You cannot trust me when I tell you of what passes on earth; how will you be able to trust me when I tell you of what passes in heaven? No man has ever gone up into heaven; but there is one who has come down from heaven, the Son of Man, who dwells in heaven. And this Son of Man must be lifted up, as the serpent was lifted up by Moses in the wilderness; so that those who believe in him may not perish, but have eternal life.

"God so loved the world, that he gave up his only-begotten Son, so that those who believe in him may not perish, but have eternal life. When God sent his Son into the world, it was not to reject the world, but so that the world might find salvation through him. For the man who believes in him, there is no rejection; the man who does not believe is already rejected; he has not found faith in the name of God's only-begotten Son. Rejection lies in this, that when the light came into the world men preferred darkness to light; preferred it, because their doings were evil. Anyone who acts shamefully hates the light, will not come into the light, for fear that his doings will be found out, so that his deeds may be seen for what they are, deeds done in God."

We will be judged on this—on our refusal of the light. Saint Paul, struck down in his body precisely by light, on the road to Damascus; Saint Paul, who saw Christ as a light, a blinding light, did not announce to the Gentiles an incomprehensible mystery to be accepted with one's eyes closed. To the Ephesians, the Romans and the Colossians, he announced the same good news: that the long-concealed mystery had just been made manifest. I have always known this and I will be judged according to my receiving or not receiving this answer which the Lord gave me.

Who is the thinking, loving creature who is on the point of landing on the stars and who will thus become a god in accordance with the promise made to Eve by the serpent? How close I feel to Nicodemus, who asked stupid questions and who, like me in everything related to technology, understood nothing! Yet he believed that the light had come into the world. Or rather, he did not have to believe it, since he had seen it. He had spent one night at the feet of the Savior. And what he heard and saw he finally understood, stupid as he was, since he repeated it, and thanks to him, the eternal word has come down to us.

I too believe in the light. I deny the mystery accepted by the modern world. I deny the absurd. I have no regard for the miracles of technology if they unfold in a materialistic prison, even if the prison has the dimension of the cosmos. I have no interest in reaching the planets if what the remote-controlled rocket carries is this poor body destined to rot away and this poor heart, which will have vainly beaten for creatures who themselves are dust and ashes. "It is this horror which creates your faith. . . ." Yes, it is true. It is not fear, in the sense given to it by Lucretius, which creates gods, but horror of the void, or rather its absurdity. The thinking man does not consent to have no thought, and the loving heart does not consent to feeling no love.

Nevertheless we are unable to create for ourselves any god. He is Someone, Someone he had not invented or imagined that Nicodemus went to see one night, in great secret, through fear of the Jews. He is Someone I did not invent, whom I also can come to at night when I do not sleep. There is no insomnia for the Christian that may not become that meeting between poor Nicodemus and the light that came into this world, a man like him, a man like us, yet who was Christ, the Son of the Father, the Lamb of God.

It is night inside me, and it was in the darkness of that night that I found Him, but not every time I wished to find Him. They are moments of grace. For some, as for Nicodemus, there has perhaps been only one meeting, only one night, but one which may have guided their entire life. Nothing in the world could make me renounce what I saw, what I heard, what I touched, even if it was only once.

I realize that this light itself constitutes a mystery, and even much more: a center of mysteries which demands faith. Nevertheless it compels recognition. This light exists in history. It illuminates and burns.

It was spread over the earth. I cherish the words of our Lord when He said: "It is fire that I have come to spread over the earth, and what better wish can I have than that it should be kindled?" It burns in words that are still burning, and it is precisely like fire that these words are transmitted. At times the fire smolders and moves slowly, and spreads through roots and turf. At other times the flame leaps from pine to pine, from treetop to treetop, and devours both the head and the heart of the burning tree of man.

This light I see, which I do not refuse; others, many others, almost all the others, reject it because they do not see it and because they deny even the possibility of seeing it. And they denounce as an illusion or as an imposture or as a mental deficiency our acceptance of this light. I cannot pretend, even through charity, to forget the accusation our Lord made against them during that night when Nicodemus listened to Him without understanding. He accused them of preferring the darkness because their works were wicked.

The light forbids our deceiving ourselves about what is evil and what is good. It causes to rise up from our confused inner world those acts which are not under the control of human justice, which no human code condemns, which, however, we recognize as being evil. That evil I must dominate and destroy in myself if I wish to be on the side of Christ.

This light confronts us with the mystery of evil as soon as we begin to experience faith. It is indeed hard to believe in this law of an original transgression of which we are heirs both innocent and guilty. It is hard to believe we are born condemned. And yet the light shows me that human nature has been wounded. I can fight against the cause which faith assigns to this wound, but not against the fact that the wound bleeds, and that it bleeds at the heart of a nature capable of love, of that very love which involves the gift of life. The light I have received, to which I have consented, made me attentive, for as long as I live, to that contradiction in myself and in all men : between infamy and holiness, between brutality and love in the same being. The man who has seen this once will see it forever. The man who has seen this cannot not raise his eyes to the light which illuminates in its profundity the mystery of evil. Who is the light? Nicodemus knew. And knowing this, despite the simplicity of his mind, he knew all the rest. Nicodemus knew that the light is Someone.

Nicodemus faintly saw this face on the night he met our Lord. Paul, on the highway, only heard a voice: "I am Jesus whom you persecute." My eyes have seen nothing, I have heard nothing, and yet I do not refuse the Mystery. I enter into it and sink into it. It envelops me and bears me up.

I am not bewildered by what it reveals to me, by all those things in me which offend the absolute purity of God, because the same word which is ceaselessly repeated in the Gospel returns more than seventy times seven in every guilty and penitent life: "Your sins are forgiven." The need to become again like a child if I wish to have some part in the Kingdom does not exist without the possibility of becoming that child again, no matter how sinful I have been. This at least comes from my own experience, and I know it is true. "How is this possible?" poor Nicodemus asked. "How can this be? How can I be born again?" Yes, indeed, how can that come about? It is through this door that a Christian of my type enters into the mystery of the sacrificed Lamb. Our sins are forgiven because Someone else assumes them. They might easily have been forgiven without the sacrifice of the Lamb, because everything is possible to God. But Saint John testifies to this: "God is love," and "There is no greater love than the laying down of one's life." The Lord Himself said this to us. The cross rises up at the point where these two words meet.

From this point on, a Christian can speak only for himself, and his experience is personal. The mystery of Jesus is the Almighty consenting to having a destiny in the totally human sense that each of us has a destiny. Think of the number of destinies that will have crossed and cut through ours between the awakening of our conscience and our heart and that descent when death is announced by a form of solitude similar to that of which Pascal speaks when he says "We die alone." No! we do not die alone. That Nazarene, born under Augustus, who died under Tiberius, will not only have crossed our destiny, but will also have penetrated it to the point of joining with it, no matter how sinful we have been.

When I was a young poet and knew by heart countless lines, I often recited to myself those which Verlaine the penitent has Christ say :

Love! Come out from your night. Love! This
    is my thought
For all eternity, poor abandoned soul,
That you had to love me, who am the last in
    your life.

I used to repeat this last phrase [*moi seul qui suis resté*] when I was young because I found it beautiful, but only today do I know it is true. Nothing remains, no one remains, no matter how filled our life is, outside those we love who belong to us, but who are so close to us as to be confused with our solitude. What is old age? An absence which is death already. A huge ebb tide leaves the creature on the sand, among parts of a wreck where names and first names, which only the creature knew, are slowly being effaced. And there is scarcely any difference between the old man in his brocaded uniform and those old farmers I used to see as a child on their doorsteps, motionless like stone statues, with their deformed hands placed on their knees. It is the same absence and the same silence. It is then that the "I am the last in your life" resounds through us like an accomplished verified prophecy. Yes, Lord, You have remained in my blood and flesh, but You are not less present in each word You have said than in the bread and wine, and You are not less present in the sick man whom the atheist treats, in the pauper he helps, and in the prisoner he visits.

O light which we love and which loves us, you burn in the dark. The Christian mystery is the darkness which makes light more plain; and it is the light which penetrates the darkness and which, without destroying it, kindles it. Three night scenes reveal the Christian life in its profundity. The first is that night I have just meditated on during which, furtively, Nicodemus, the good Pharisee, came in great secret to listen to the Lord, who was still living and militant, and who, in a hurry to bring it to an end, quickly threw fire on the ground. The second was the night on Gethsemane when the light which had come into the world was only a wretched Jew, deserted even by his friends, even by his Father; and the only flames burning in that cold spring night were the torches of the revelers. The night of agony which will last until the end of the world. The night which the true friends of the Lord have always preferred was Pascal's. The words Pascal heard during that night from the twenty-third to the twenty-fourth of November I also heard in my adolescence, and everything was changed for me. Even if I have sacrificed nothing, and renounced nothing, and fell asleep in pleasure, at least I never lost the sense of the presence, within a stone's throw, of that innocent crushed in the blind dark night under the weight of the human crime he assumed.

The third night was first a twilight on a deserted road between Jerusalem and Emmaus. It is the night agreeable to my weakness and to the fear I have of death. And as the darkness grew around the three men walking along that road, what burned in the early night were the hearts of the disciple called Cleophas and of his companion. "Were not our souls ardent as he explained the Scriptures to us?" They pushed open a door and went into a house which might have been an inn. Perhaps the room they went into was lighted only by the fire in the hearth. But I know the source from which the light came forth: from the broken bread, from the piece of bread He gave them to eat, from His holy venerable hands, the hands of a man condemned to death where the mark of the nails was still visible. "And they recognized Him when He broke bread."

I too understood at the breaking of the bread that everything was true. The most impenetrable and the strangest Mystery we are all witness to, who have kept the faith; and it is the strangeness of this Mystery that has helped us to believe all the rest. The Eucharist interrupts all our objections and refusals, all the grumblings of our reason which revolts. Everything yields to the silence within us until there is nothing left for us except to sigh, as Thomas called Didymus did, "My Lord and my God."

IV

❂ ❂ ❂

The demands of purity

�֎ �֎ ✦

COULDN'T IT BE that this Lord and this God, whom I claim as mine, and because of whom I affirm a possession so strangely impassioned, answers a need of my nature, a demand that is strong enough to create its own object? Countless times I have formulated this objection to myself. I call upon a savior because I need salvation, and I need salvation because I find myself guilty, and I find myself guilty because I believe evil is in the world and in me and that my human nature has been affected by it.

The first line of a work entitled *What I Believe* should have been: I believe that evil exists and I judge what evil is in the light of Christ. From that point, I advance along a road more deserted each day. Of all the Beatitudes in the Sermon on the

Mount, the most scorned by our day is that which is promised to the pure in heart. That demand of Christ which is in direct opposition to nature is today—as in the days of Tiberius, Claudius and Nero—in direct opposition to the world for which Christ refused to pray and which today sanctifies nature as it did two thousand years ago.

I believe that evil is in the world, but do I believe that it was not here at the very beginning and that at one moment in time it was here suddenly as a result of a deliberate act accomplished by Homo sapiens?

I leave to others the choice of hypotheses concerning what the Bible story conceals: Does it apply in reality to a single couple (this would be unthinkable), or do Adam and Eve incarnate a human continuity? But the belief that evil is in the world and at the secret part of our being, that it is born where the spirit and the flesh meet in me, is an evidence which can no more be denied than one can claim to accept the Gidian thesis that Evil is Good and that Good is Evil.

Among all the things I believe, purity of the heart more than any other isolates me in the world where this belief has become inconceivable.

I should not touch on this subject of the purity of

youth. And first, because of my age. When one has passed through the storm-ridden sea and reached the harbor, it is unsuitable to preach to those who are still struggling or who have just begun to struggle.

Yet I realize that this objection does not really hold. An old man is never over difficulties of this kind. Old age brings no solution for those who do not have the peace of God. When it is pointed toward eternity close at hand, old age risks being a period of redoubled testing because the imagination in an old man is substituted in a horrible way for what nature refuses him. The conversation of my contemporaries is often more salacious than the conversation of young men. If old age is not saintly, it is obsessional.

So, old as I am, and Christian to the best of my efforts, age is not enough to relieve me of the duty of saying to a young man: You should be pure.

But now I see another objection which concerns me alone. I was born long ago, in a very unusual place where ideas were at the opposite pole from the ideas which are current today concerning sexual matters. I have remained too close to the child I was for such a subject to inspire in me words which today a young man cannot listen to without smiling.

The child I was. . . . I was the last son of a mother who had been widowed very young, who had entered upon widowhood as seriously as one enters a convent and who looked upon herself as responsible literally for my eternal destiny. At that time, the purity of the heart and body was not one of the Christian virtues. It was synonymous with Virtue. When people said *virtue, saintly virtue,* they meant purity. Scruples of scrupulous souls were crystallized around failures of that kind. Today it is difficult to conceive of that world before Freud.

Repressions, complexes. . . . When I was a child, those training us could never have imagined the danger such evil words define. The virtue of childhood and adolescence consisted in ignoring such matters, in not referring to them, and even in not thinking of them. The mere thought of them was enough to hurl you into the abyss. It was far better not to speak of them, not to think of them and to ignore one's own body. We had to live united with a wild beast whom it was important not to know. It was reminiscent of a Spartan child and the fox hidden under the garment. The extent of our defenses and the precautions taken against ourselves I will not relate for fear of making you laugh. Actually there was nothing to laugh about.

This education in purity I underwent had little

effect on most children. They were like ducklings:
the water never wet their feathers. On the other
hand, the consequences were serious for oversensi-
tive boys. For certain types, repressions and complexes are very serious. They can be of great use in
the formation of what is called a Catholic novelist,
and enrich a successful career as writer. God alone
knows what it actually cost the beneficiary.

In other words, I am totally unable to imagine
the meaning of purity for young Christians today,
who are so different from what I was, young men
to whom everything was revealed at the age of
reason despite the precautions of their educators,
and who were saturated from childhood on in an
atmosphere created by the movies. Blood and sex,
carnal possession, tortured, mutilated flesh: a child
in the large cities today walks along the street
between posters on which the human body and
especially sexuality are exalted. The subjects are not
courage and strength but violence and crime. In
this world as it exists, it is less important for the
educator to protect the child than to warn and arm
him.

What I believe implies a disturbance which comes
from a contradiction between the Christian law, its
demand for such a singular purity over which it has
never made a compromise, and the law and demands

of nature and the gigantic complicity it finds in the outer world. At moments of confusion and despondency, I have felt exiled from a simple normal life and from what constitutes happiness for other men.

But I knew at those moments what I have always known: that gesture of impurity, that act of impurity are not like other gestures and other acts. That desire is not like our other desires. I am not concerned here with the moral or religious aspect of the problem. For many men—for those who are sensuous by nature and for those (fewer than is usually believed) who are dominated by the passions of the heart—the problem is how not to be devoured by the animal part of their nature. For the pagan, the art of living consists in using one's body and not abusing it. But this is the point: the sexual act has no resemblance to any other act: its demands are frenzied and participate in infinity. It is a tidal wave able to cover everything and bear away everything. "What does that matter? We are free to take the risk. . . ." But in taking this risk we are not alone. We involve many other creatures. It is not my intention to wax sentimental over the girls sacrificed to wicked boys. In the world of the young who pursue one another, it is often the boy who is pursued. At the end of our life, faces come back to us from our youth. There are many tears we would

5 0

like to dry, and suffering ghosts from whom we would like to ask forgiveness. Those who have loved us have suffered from all this, and we will never know how much. Each one of us will be asked this and we will be judged on this.

But if everything is to end in death, there is no risk which is important in this attraction of one creature for another, in the desire to love and be loved and to possess what one loves. Love is infinitely more than pleasure. What man and what woman, if they have truly loved, even against all rules and laws, can regret it and blush at it and not think of it except as the one moment in their lives when they lived? And it is indeed true that nothing is important in this world except love. I have no trouble in agreeing, since it is love, that it is our love which demands that we Christians be pure. It is the sole reason for our madness.

I am not a moralist. I do not believe in morality as such. We love Someone who said "Blessed are the pure in heart. . . ." We love Someone who said "Unless you become like little children again, you shall not enter my Kingdom." We love Someone who said to pluck out our eye if our eye offend us.

This Someone, whose demands are such, we love more than we perhaps realize. We have to come to the end of our life to know this. All other loves have disappeared. We are alone with God. "I who am the last in your life. . . ." This is an experienced truth for the Christian: Impurity separates us from God. The spiritual life obeys laws as verifiable as those of the physical world. Even that monster of impurity that Rimbaud was knew it and claimed that he was cut off by almost nothing from the truth "which perhaps surrounds us with its angels weeping!" And suddenly came this cry: "O purity! Purity! This moment of awakening gave me the vision of purity. It is by the spirit one goes to God! Harrowing misfortune!"

Purity is the condition for a higher love—for a possession superior to all possessions: that of God. Yes, this is what is at stake, and nothing less. And if this is not the case, why are we forbidden that from which all others derive happiness?

The possession of God does not concern only the saints and mystics. The humblest Christian, provided he has the beginning of love which is necessary for forgiveness, according to the catechism I was taught, is capable of knowing God. I have so little scorn for what men call love that I see nothing and no one who deserves to be sacrificed to it, except love itself, the love which lives, the love which is the real name of God: "God is Love."

This is the meaning of *Le soulier de satin*. Indeed, Claudel in this story assigns a lofty place to human love. What joins Prouhèze with Rodrigue is truly the divine part of their being, which calls out to itself and seeks itself and yearns to possess itself. And yet that part which Prouhèze is unwilling to sacrifice—she has not the strength to do this—she is willing to be separated from by grace, willing that an abyss be created between her and her beloved. If Prouhèze had given herself to Rodrigue, their love affair would have ended like all love affairs in the routine of habit, in boredom, in disgust perhaps and perhaps in hate. We possess forever the creature we have given up.

Our heart, our poor heart full of the creature we have loved or desired, gives her up, but not in exchange for nothing. We give her in exchange for a priceless pearl which each one of us sinners can hold in his clenched fist.

You are loved for what you are, just as when you love someone, the worst part of his character attracts you the most at times: his defects are more appealing than the virtues of virtuous men. This is the way the Creator loves His creature. The same Lord who has such harsh words on impurity: "If your eye offend you, pluck it out . . . ," or on the creators of scandal: "He had better have been drowned, with a millstone hung about his neck," this same Lord has only words of mercy and pardon for the woman taken in adultery, for the woman of Samaria, for the woman to whom much was forgiven because of her great love. These are classic examples. But each time when, in the Gospel, the Lord says "Your sins are forgiven you . . . ," he obliterates with a single word, with a single glance, all the wretched abominations of a man's life, abominations which, in every period, in all men and all women, are always the same.

I realize, of course, that all sinners are not alike, and that some sins are more serious than others. But if Saint Paul points this out by denouncing certain abominations as abominable, the Lord says to us: "Blessed are the pure in heart." He tells us to recover the spirit of childhood and he tells it to us all. He does not judge that point from which each of us has to begin moving toward Him. Courtesans will enter the Kingdom ahead of us. We do not know what real sin is, what real impurity is. In some tormented souls there is an obscenity of false purity. They forget that the most monstrous part of us is almost always inherited and not acquired.

The Christian marriage, no matter how much affection joins the couple, is not a remedy against lust. It is a wall we erect between ourselves and that lust which, in some, goes far beyond the sexual act and cannot be appeased in marital life, because it involves the attraction of unknown creatures and the taste for adventure and chance meetings. It is an evil which does not affect all of us. What we must recognize is the fact that a Christian marriage simplifies nothing in the problem of purity, and that within that problem it creates a world of difficulties which concern it alone.

Suddenly I feel a scruple. I am yielding to the obsession of the age and am speaking like a man of today who has no doubt concerning the primary of sex. In reality, all of us are not consecrated to great passions, and none of our moralists has ever said anything more accurate than La Rochefoucauld: "How many men would never have loved, if they had never heard of love!" It is true that we are born predisposed to the adventures of the heart or, on the contrary, not highly endowed for passion.

This is the same thing as saying the problem is different for each of us. In the sexual problem there are only individual truths. Each of us has or has had his drama. Or his drama was that of not having a drama. Many have had no other happiness save the insipid happiness of men without a story. And many have been obsessed all their lives by a desire, possessed by a hunger they have resisted, against which they have fought, or on the contrary to which they have become enslaved, and the need to satisfy and indulge this desire was their sole preoccupation. It makes little difference whether they triumphed over it or were possessed by it: their entire life was colored by that secret passion, which was either declared or repressed. And everything else seems insipid to them and of no concern to them, everything that is not a certain face, a certain being, always the same which they look for all their lives in each creature they meet. There are only individual stories and individual dramas: "All these human bodies are stories of solitude!"

But all these solitary lives, all these unique and different problems rise up for Christians from the same grace and the same love. Christ answers the question asked by each one of our lives. If your heart is empty, He is here to fill it. If it is obsessed by some unworthy person whose possession tends to vilify us, Christ is ready to substitute Himself in a sovereign and absolute way for that hunger and thirst, to substitute another thirst and another hunger.

Purity is not a negative virtue. It does not consist in following the moral rules of a niggling prudish master who spies on our every glance and forces us

to keep holding in our hand Tartuffe's handker-
chief. We have to be pure because the Lord wants
this and because His love does not allow any sharing.
But we have to be pure also in order to give ourselves to others, for Christ's love is love for others:
"For I was hungry, and you gave me food, naked,
and you clothed me, a prisoner, and you came to
me." No Christian today looks upon the Christian
life solely from the viewpoint of individual salvation which dominated the system of education I
underwent. The giving of ourself is the vocation of
all of us. In order to give oneself to the souls of
others, we have to give up their bodies, except the
one with which we are called upon to form one
body. It is a harsh law, which does not however exile
us from love. On the contrary, it joins us with love
and establishes our life on a double spiritual conquest: our own conquest first, and then the conquest
of those whom the Lord puts on our path, not in
order that we take advantage of them but in order
that we save them.

And if this vocation seems too sublime to a young
man, if the knowledge he has of himself, of his body
with its demands and passions, discourages him
from attempting an effort at domination and self-
mastery, he should not allow himself to be impressed
by our wretchedness and the failures which are

repeated throughout our poor lives. God is Love. And the One who took on our flesh, who became flesh, knows all the snares it sets for us. The lack of balance in us created by the alliance of a body whose sensuousness is so blind and powerful with a soul made for God was tested by the One who, being a man, was also the Son of God.

Above all, we should not scorn the flesh. It is not the enemy I was taught to be ashamed of and to be afraid of when I was a child. This body of ours was sanctified by the Son of Man who Himself took it on and it is sanctified by the presence of the soul which enters it, which is able to receive God—and not only that, but if it maintains a state of grace, if it remains pure, can literally overflow with Him, yes, overflow with God, according to the promise which has been made to us: "If a man has any love for me, he will be true to my word; and then he will win my Father's love, and we will both come to him, and make our continual abode with him." And it is sanctified by the small Host, by the Lamb of God, as often as our heart speaks to us of this.

The flesh humiliates us. That is perhaps the means by which it can serve us the best. But it should not arouse despair in us. There is in us a purity of desire which is seen by the One who measures better than we do the part of heredity and what belongs to pathology, and all that makes us understand more clearly, when we think of it, the look of affection and pity with which the Lord embraces all Marys and all lepers. He has harsh words only for the hypocritical Scribes and Pharisees, not for sinners. I have always been moved by what I read of Abbé Huvelin, the vicar of Saint Augustine, who converted and guided Père de Foucauld, and who wanted to absolve every man he met.

We Catholics have within our reach this source of forgiveness. It keeps us from being sucked into the mire. It gives us the measurement of what the Lord meant when He said we have to forgive more than seventy times seven—because He remits our suffering and obliterates it. He has already paid up for it. No matter how heavy our past, we have given it over to His mercy. The older I grow and the closer I move to the last shore, the more easily I can measure with my eyes all that has been accumulated in a long life, if it has been honorable in terms of the world, and the more easily I can measure as a writer the responsibility of every being who speaks and writes and influences the minds of people, and, if a novelist, his influence on the imagination, on the heart, on the heart that is flesh.

And yet the closer I come to that terrible day of

reckoning, the less I fear it, because the love of God which is in us has been given to us by Him. This love comes to us from Him and is the irrefutable testimonial that we ourselves are loved and therefore forgiven. And even if we do not feel this love, if it remains completely within our will, if we move ahead into the night and touch, as the poor woman did, the hem of the robe—and the Lord does not turn around—that love also should be enough to reassure us. The sentimental does not count as much as what is lived. What we do for Christ is what counts.

At the ending of our life, there is no greater happiness than to have loved Him. The young man's fidelity to Christ is paid for a hundred times over by the fidelity of the old man he will be one day. That day which seems so far off to him. To me, my youth seems close indeed! It seems to me that yesterday I was one of those boys. I have no trouble in imagining their lives and their difficulties, their enthusiasms and unexpected wild ideas, and at certain moments their temptations to upset everything and accept no other law save that of desire. But it is not desire, it is purity or at least the effort and the fight we wage in order to preserve or win it back which makes conquerors of us.

V

❀ ❀ ❀

Enemy brothers

❀ ❀ ❀

THOSE WHO wear themselves out during their life-
time in this conquest for purity of heart and who
have fought up to the beginnings of old age, and
sometimes throughout advanced old age, against the
flesh and its passions, even if their numbers are
reduced today, should recognize one another by this
sign and know that they are brothers, and love one
another even as they have received the commandment for this love. Yes, they should be recognized
by the affection they feel for one another. The
pagans used to say about the first disciples of the
Lord: "See how they love one another!" How far
we have moved from that state! For a long time I
believed, and I still believe, that the religious instinct is at its inception a horror for that solitude

which deepens for every creature as he advances toward death. The age of love is the time of the illusion that someone else can be confused with us and that we can be two, until the day when Newman's "my Creator and myself" expresses the only meeting which is at the same time a communion and more than a communion: "It is not I who live but Christ who liveth in me."

But the religion which "joins us with God" joins the faithful one with the other. It should join them together. A Christian, even without a family and friends, belongs to a family and has his special place in a gathering. He has fathers, brothers and sisters. Each day he can sit down at the Lord's table. Yes, each morning, if he feels so inclined. If it were that joy of being no longer alone which had attracted me to the Church, I state now that this would not have kept me there. I can speak only for myself, and it is possible that others, many others, do not feel what I have felt all my life within the visible Church: a sentiment of redoubled human solitude.

Through my own fault, I am sure. I have never, at any moment in my life, been truly associated with the life of a parish such as that which I admire from the outside at Saint-Séverin, or at Saint-Sulpice, or at Saint Germain-des-Prés. I have been incapable of participating and have always disliked it. At school I was the one who refused to take part in games and was looked upon, because of that, as being surly. My instinct always kept me outside of the flock. In this I am guilty and I confess that I have been the creator of my own solitude within the Christian flock.

But when I move outside the magic impassable circle which my own temperament has drawn around me and which has condemned me, Christian that I am, to grow old and die alone, I see and ascertain and test the fact that the flock of the faithful is in reality a flock of juxtaposed solitary lives and not only solitary lives but hostile enemy worlds.

What I believe is not necessarily what brings me consolation. What I believe, and what I know, arise from an incomprehensible mystery. We share in the same Christ, in the same breaking of Living Bread. And we remain as unknown to one another as if it were in a public bus and not at the Lord's table that we had knelt side by side. And if only that was all we were: unknown to one another! Too often we have been enemies to the point of violence and hate and murder. The same baptism and the same Eucharist serve nowise to diminish by a millimeter the abyss separating a positivist of the Maurras ilk from a liberal worker-priest. What I believe is here in conflict with what I am affirming and testing.

This opposition has always existed in the Church between two types of minds whose differing demands are not, however, contradictory. These two demands can be summarized in two words: the repository and the message. There is revealed truth defined in the words of the creed and established in the dogmas protected by the Church, and there is the good news to be told to all nations.

All of us know this: that if we are part of Christ and belong to the Roman Catholic Apostolic Church, we incline toward one direction or the other. On the extreme right, frowning theologians have an aggressive orthodoxy and hold the repository of revelation in a sealed vase and yearn to transmit it exactly as they received it, and therefore preserve it from all contamination. It is clearly true that these men are distrustful by nature, and hostile to whatever is undertaken by minds on the other side. On that side are those who, guided less by the idea of a repository than by the idea of a message, do not emphasize definitions or traditions or usages made venerable by time but believe that every period, and ours perhaps more than any other, is waiting for the message and hoping for the message.

Thus, within the Church, the holders of the repository are opposed to the holders of the message. Yet I do not believe that this opposition constitutes the real problem. The two tendencies are legitimate and both correspond to the vocation of the visible Church. Where then is the scandal? Because there is a scandal, and I have no intention of denying it.

We should confront the opposition and, more than the opposition, the insurmountable hostility which aligns some against others— and I do not mean Christians of different confessions, but within the Church itself, Catholics against Catholics. I am not thinking of quarrels among theologians. I am only concerned with their political tendency, because it is true that every theological conviction entails a political attitude.

This evidence comes first to mind: At times I can feel closer to a believer, to a pious man, who is at a great distance from my own Church. This is merely a paradox in appearance. When I am with a Moslem or a Jew, if they are devout, I know in advance, before they have said a word, what separates me from them. To some degree I understand the abyss between us. There can be no surprise in this encounter. But what is unfamiliar to me, and what delights me when I discover them, is suddenly the words of praise which I recognize, the prayer which might have come from my own heart, the love for the Father who is in Heaven, and at times, and even with certain Jews, the attraction they feel for Christ.

On the too-infrequent occasions when I have had the privilege of meeting a true Israelite or a holy Moslem, I think of all the dwellings there are in my Father's House. And what I feel with respect to a son of Israel or a son of the Prophet I feel still more—needless to say—with Christians of different confessions who participate in Christ, with those of my separated brothers who have a living faith, or with certain souls who do not belong to any definite confession, who live, as Simone Weil lived, just outside the Church, and the light which pierces them, which they refract, illuminates me all the more perhaps because it is not expressed in traditional formulas. In them grace appears in its elemental state outside all those ways which for us are the customary channels. It is somewhat similar to our discovery of strangers who know and love as we do a secret spot in the forest which was the goal of our lonely walks. We are surprised that they found it by other paths which we did not know existed.

The culminating goal where meet all those who tend toward contemplation, in the same dark night of a Saint John of the Cross, no matter how far apart they be at their starting point, moves me less than those encounters halfway along with separated brothers of all races and confessions, and at times even with avowed militant atheists who, outside of any temporal interest, are looking for the Kingdom of God and His justice, in whom I recognize all the signs of the charity of that Christ they do not know.

This is a law of my mind. It is a terrible reversal when I feel closer to a believer the farther away he is from the visible Church to which I belong. Yes, I feel more distant from and more hostile to certain men whom I see professing the same creed as I do and kneeling at the same table and sharing the same Bread.

But here again the paradox is only apparent. I will never admit, and no one in the world will ever make me admit it, that the Christian is free in his political choices, that he is free to choose the methods he adopts in order to make them triumph. In France a large number of Catholics believe this, and not only those who carry out their religious duties mechanically, Catholics of the eleven-o'clock Mass who perform certain gestures but have no authentic religious life. The believers I have in mind are practicing and devout, and it is in the degree to

which they are practicing that I feel with respect to
them not only a stranger but hostile. If a Soviet
officer lays hands on a human being and tortures a
prisoner, I can consider this act repulsive, but it does
conform with the idea the officer has concerning the
human person and his absolute subordination to the
interests of the Communist Party and the Russia
of the Soviets. If, on the other hand, a Christian,
who through the week has recourse to certain
methods of forcing suspects to speak, piously takes
communion on Sunday, surrounded by his children,
it is that communion which drastically separates me
from him and makes him a stranger and an enemy
to me.

You say very few practicing Christians practice
torture? But there are thousands and millions who,
if they don't approve of it, at least understand and
excuse it. And there are thousands and millions,
even among the devout, who come close to hating
and despising Jews, or if they don't hate and despise
them at least look upon them in their status of Jews
as a race under suspicion, and in the same way too
often look upon Arabs in their status of Arabs. This
would not shock me in the least if we were talking
of agnostics or atheists, of men like Barrès or Maurras. For me the scandal begins only with the faith

when it is practiced and experienced within the Church by Christians even more faithful than I am myself, as I have been often and justly reproached for, more charitable, more devoted to good works than I am myself.

At this point it seems to me impossible not to go beyond the notion of diversity. There is much more than diversity among Catholics within Catholicism. It is a matter of an absolute irreducible contradiction, at least for a mind like my own. I realize what reasons would be given me by a convinced Catholic of Maurras tendencies. He would show me that in reality the Christian message is indissolubly bound up with the defense of Western civilization. What I am claiming is the uselessness of the efforts we might make to dissolve the hostility of minds within the Church, which breaks out with even more scandal because they are fervent Christians.

What can be done? Should we despair of that unity for which the Son of Man once prayed to His Father? I would say no. But I believe it necessary to move toward that unity beyond the visible boundaries of the Church.

Within the Church, it is already in a certain way accomplished, thanks to the creed we recite together and the Bread broken for all. The enemy brothers *are, if not reconciled, at least kneeling side by side in a kind of permanent "truce of God" of which our churches are the privileged setting, even in the most troubled periods. We are so accustomed to this that no longer do we pay any attention to it. We join with one another beyond everything that divides us on the earth in the One who will unite us all, and somehow in spite of ourselves, within His Love.

I know that this outer peace reigns at the communion table only because we do not speak to this unknown brother who is partaking beside us. When for years you attend the same chapel and the same Mass, you make friends about whom you know nothing, you become attached to a child who takes communion, like an angel, close beside you. You see him grow up into an adolescent, and then suddenly he disappears from your life where he had held no other place save that of an angel on your left or on your right at the moment of communion. Sometimes I tell myself that that angel to whom I never spoke and to whom I had become attached and for whom I had prayed has perhaps become a leader of the plastics industry. Nevertheless for years we had broken Bread together, with the Lord between us and in us.

There is nothing else to expect, nothing else to

hope for, save that kneeling side by side of antagonistic spirits who however participate, each one separately, in the divine spirit. For everything is possible to God and even, since He is Love, it is possible not to take into account the signs of idolatry in one of the faithful, be the idol race or nation.

But we cannot be satisfied with this simple exterior unity. I am one of those who believe that the real unity lies beyond the visible frontiers of Holy Church at that ideal point defined by the Lord Himself on that day among days when He sat down on the edge of a well and spoke to an adulterous woman who had come to draw water. "The time is coming, nay, has already come, when true worshipers will worship the Father in spirit and in truth." Worshipers in spirit and in truth are to be found in all confessions and all Churches, and they are recognizable by a sign, and they love one another, in a manner of speaking, not in spite of what separates them but in some way or other because of what separates them. The miracle is that, being separated as they are, they recognize one another and join with one another, and they see that they come from the same spirit.

I hope I am not misunderstood. For I still believe with all my heart that the Catholic Church our mother is the true Church and that it is always Peter in Rome who binds and unbinds. But I believe that the spirit it has in superabundance extends far beyond its visible frontiers and that the Lord recognizes Himself in some way in worshipers belonging to other flocks, to other sheepfolds.

The huge disaster of colonial wars was to compromise those first gropings of minds looking for one another and recognizing one another. But at the end, we will succeed in moving out from that long night. The seed sown by the Benedictines of Toumliline or by the Little Brothers of Père Foucauld will fructify one day. If God gives us the grace to see peace return, to see the reconciliation of races, we will take up again on site what once we understood with the people of North Africa, with those who do not know that Jesus is the Christ but who know that we have a Father in Heaven and who worship Him as we do, with the same words we use.

Unity could be accomplished more naturally with them than with those of our Catholic brothers, who are fervent Catholics but who believe that politics has its laws and its morality and that it enjoys an absolute autonomy even with regard to God.

And yet, the commandment does not allow any misunderstanding : We must love in God our enemy brothers. What is the real meaning of this expression "to love one another in God?" To love in God those brothers whose methods and goals it is impossible for us not to loathe, and who themselves loathe everything concerning us, may well be an easy verbal way of avoiding the difficulty. What positive and efficacious effort can all of us put into a will to reunite outside of a feeling of dislike which can develop into hatred, alas, and even into murder? For murder has become the daily bread of France.

No matter what our political opinions may be, all of us believe that to love one another in God, even our enemies, expresses a reality and corresponds to a possibility. We would not be Christians if we challenged our Lord's absolute command, love your enemies. We must therefore begin by desiring it, and truly desiring it, in order to desire it efficaciously. And if the first condition is to ask it of the Lord as a grace, the second is to try to reach it by human means.

But first, there is a very consoling truth which you discover at my age, even if you have been as combative as I have been, even if you have vigorously taken sides and have made a commitment as I have continued to make. We discover that in reality we do not detest the men we think we detest and that the opposite is true: they do not detest us. We often confuse hate with exasperation. These are two very different states. We exasperate one another throughout our lives, that is true, because we do not take into account the reasons of the other man. Then, at the end of our life, when the dust of long-past fights has settled down, we meet by chance a former enemy. We are surprised at the pleasure of being together, of speaking of past oppositions, of friends or enemies in the time of our youth who are no longer with us. It seems then that the Lord Himself speaks softly to us: "Don't you see now, my children, that you don't hate one another? It is literally true that you didn't hear one another. Each of you was deaf to the arguments of the other. It is possible you never felt real hatred."

It is one of the blessings of old age, and even of an old age as belligerent as my own, to open our eyes to what should be for us Christians the most reassuring of evidences: namely, that irritation and exasperation are not hate, and that if real hate is almost always absolute and insurmountable, it is not the same thing with the impulses of our feelings. In that situation, there is a method we must find in order to explain ourselves to the enemy and appease him and have him listen to us.

Pascal, who has said everything, proposes in this often-quoted sentence a rule for us to follow: "When we wish to resume an argument efficaciously, and show to someone that he is wrong, we should point out from what angle he is considering the matter, because ordinarily it is true from that angle, and confess this truth to him, but also to reveal to him the angle from which it is false."

There is no need to reflect on this very long in order to see the defect in the armor, although it is Pascal's armor, and one which is very obvious. Pascal concedes to the enemy that there is an angle from which he is right, but he does not imagine that there may be an angle from which he himself might be wrong. Yet it is to the degree that we admit not only that the enemy may be right, partially from his viewpoint, but to the willingness we also admit that we ourselves are capable of error, that we will move in his direction and that he will consent to move toward us.

The fact is that in politics, if ideas are in conflict, they can yield to reasoning. But they are passions, and of all passions the most furious, the most blind, and therefore the least capable of complying with reason.

But our passion for unity is not blind. The true

unity to which we aspire is that of Christians who recognize one another by their belief that for them there is no other legitimate politics in the world than that which tends to inscribe in the history of mankind the will of the Father who is in Heaven. Each of the beatitudes of the Sermon on the Mount concerns our entire life and therefore our life of a citizen. We should try to inscribe them in our deeds, outside of any nationalism, or racial hate, or spirit of conquest.

No other politics is permitted a Christian save the search for the Kingdom of God and His justice. Neither is he allowed to turn aside from the conflicts dividing his brothers. He must remain above the confusion and also within the confusion. We are of those whom the love of Christ and hope in His reign have not cut off from human activity, from that sinister daily history we call politics. This solid participation, within time, of souls who live only for the eternal seem to me the meeting point of those who want to be one, as the Father, Son and Holy Spirit are one.

We know with certainty that the first Christian communities paid no heed to the problems arising from the Roman occupation or the politics of Herod. But they were expecting the return of the Lord on a day close at hand and had no doubt that history would be accomplished. It is because time takes forever to come to an end, and because Christ did not come (as the first Christians believed He would) to terminate the criminal history of men, but came to penetrate and transform it from within, because for the Lord a day is the same as a thousand years and a thousand years as a day. We are still the first Christians and we have learned not to separate the search for the Kingdom of God from its accomplishment in this sweet kingdom of the earth, as Bernanos used to say, which would already be the Kingdom of God if men had accepted the teaching which was given them on the holy mountain.

We answered the question which Etienne Borne asked one day: Is there a politics of the Sermon on the Mount? It seems to me now that the worshipers in spirit and truth of the Father are joined and consummate their unity in the assurance that it does exist. This participation of the eternal within the temporal would have resulted in the temporal solution of problems which seem insoluble to us. Judged by the present-day French drama, it is obvious that a politics inspired by Christian humanism would have spared us bloodshed, would have reduced the number of our crimes, protected us from a shame to which we succumb at times, and maintained our prestige in the midst of those people who once loved us.

The feeling we all have of being witnesses to a twilight with no promise of dawn, the horror which fills our hearts at times that this Christian civilization of the West, so rich in works of all kinds and which, in spite of so many crimes, has done so much for the reign of Christ and given such laudable examples of holiness, that this civilization has started its decline and is at every moment threatened with being wiped out with one blow,—this feeling, we must agree, makes it hard for us to practice the faith that we must nevertheless nurture within, faith in the unity of all men in Christ! We cannot, as Saint Augustine could in his last days, when the Roman world was collapsing everywhere, see in the barbarians about to take us over a gigantic harvest of men promised to the Church. Because ours are not barbarians. These enemies of the West were once Christians and are no longer. They knew Christ and refused Him. They have decreed the death of God.

Whose fault is this? Is there any possible doubt? The truth of the matter is that Western Christianity has failed in its vocation. It is to be blamed for not evangelizing or for evangelizing only halfway. God needed men, and men exploited God. That is the crux of the matter.

On first examination, the unity toward which we should strive seems impossible for two reasons. First, within the Church and facing the rising danger, each party violently reacts in an opposite direction; and then outside, where the huger Marxist force tends to annihilate whatever is Christian because it is the most hated thing in the world and the most hostile.

And yet faith is all we need to maintain our courage. In the world as we find it, we believe that Christ is present and that His invisible presence is felt in it. A nonbeliever said to me that what had struck him most in Moscow were the churches crowded with people praying. Whatever happens, even in a world three-quarters blotted out by a weapon of destruction, there will always be in the back part of some cellar a small group crowding around a table and a man anointed who breaks and distributes the Living Bread.

That is the unity already brought about, the unity of the mustard seed concentrating all the harvests of future time which already today conceals the last harvest: the one in which will be consummated the separation of the good from the bad seed.

In that day, when the Son of Man has returned and when all the grain is stored up in the granary of the Father of the family, we will understand that the unity we aspired to almost desperately already existed without our knowing it at the time when our miserable life was torn by unruly passions, and had been accomplished in spite of us and without us.

VI

❂ ❂ ❂

Tom Thumb

※ ※ ※

HAD I LIVED the life of a practical man, of a militant within an active parish, I am sure that a certain form of solitude would not have developed in me and that it would not even have been affected by human and religious relationships carried on with my brothers. That solitude is a part of every man, but in a man of my type, it remains conscious, at the very center of destiny, like a kernel around which it crystallized and took form—my destiny of a writer, of a believer and of a Catholic. I have been inspired in the domain of literary creation, and in the realm of prayer, because I have been alone and because my solitude has had no other remedy save that of writing in this world and of knowing God in the next. But first in this world where He was incarnate and where He lived and still remains.

This meditation on what I believe will have helped me to understand the first cause of my faith, in the human sense: this solitude which might for an agnostic appear to be the obvious sufficient reason for what must be called my bias, my prejudice with regard to God, the requirement felt by all sensitive souls which finds no other appeasement save that given to them at the dawn of life when their mother held them in her arms. As soon as they were taken from her, they found themselves in the meanness of sexuality, where the affection of a child resembles a little girl who has been insulted, soiled and driven to despair. I recognize in myself this affection which is an ally of God, but I swear that it has developed around a reality, and this is the point I will insist on before ending this meditation.

A critical mind developed in me quite early. I can see clearly in this the presence of my father, whom I did not know and who was a nonbeliever. When I take pen in hand, the scholars awaken in me a form of zest and maliciousness which I perhaps inherited. It is true that my pious mother marked me forever as a Christian, but her religious training, which was captious, very early forced my reason to object. There was a good chance that my mind, in following its natural bent, would have been repulsed by the religion I had been taught. At eighteen, I took pleasure in reading Anatole France, and precisely the anticlerical Anatole France, author of *L'Anneau d'améthyste*. Through it I freed myself from a long-standing constraint. I was convinced that the Christian atmosphere which had surrounded my childhood deserved this mockery. The contradiction between the Gospels and the social-political convictions of the avaricious bourgeoisie which had no sense whatsoever of justice (it had shown this in the Dreyfus case) seemed to me flagrant. The solution I thought I had found in *Le Sillon** of Marc Sangnier was condemned by the Church, which blocked this way out, as it seemed to destroy by the encyclical *Pascendi* everything that would have permitted such a student as myself to harmonize his belief with the currents of modern thought. This was the compromise which the encyclical, in clear terms, had condemned.

The more I think of it, the clearer it appears to me that the loss of faith, under the conditions of my life of that time and in spite of my hidden affection famished and insatiable, should have taken place in me as in so many others. And if this never came about, in spite of my rebellion and irritation and

* See Introduction, p. xii.

mockery, it is because at every moment of my destiny, and even at those moments when my religious life had reached its lowest ebb, when the river was only a tiny stream, even then I held in my closed fist, despite its small size, a pearl of great value, as it is written, something hard, luminous, unique and precious, something for which I find only the banal adjective *ineffable*.

One stone, one hard fact. Despite the extensiveness of its legend or of its myth, as people prefer to say today—and the apprentice historian I was did not fail to do this, and many of his readings related to this problem—sufficient history remained in the New Testament for me to have no doubt that that man had really existed and that his basic words were reported there. He had truly said them, and I was the living proof and witness that they were spirit and life. I lived on them, and in the most physical sense I was nourished on them. They saved me from despair in those struggles which every man goes through, and at those hours when in the dark forest I could barely make out the light that Tom Thumb (having lost his way, in the engraving of Gustave Doré I was fond of) discovers from the top of the tall tree he climbed. But the door against which Tom Thumb finally collapsed was never, in the tale of my own life, that of the ogre. It was the house of one man among all men, the only one who gave forth the gentleness which all the others had refused me, a gentleness that was strong and without affectation, and which only a God has the power to join with infinite force. I would go in and sit down at the table of the inn. But to stay there I would have to be pure. And how could I remain pure with my young body? So I would go in, and then leave. I would sin once more. But no matter how far away I was from the house, I was sure of seeing its light again if I climbed a treetop.

Many other Tom Thumbs, lost in the evil forest, have seen a light, but even if it was not the house of the ogre, neither was it for most of them the house of Emmaus. "A light came into the world and the world received it not." We come back to the words Nicodemus heard. This also I believe. I believe that the world refuses the light. That it is free to refuse it is the nature of Love. But does it choose in full knowledge? Is it always a question of free choice? This is not the place to examine the mysteries of freedom. Yes, the mysteries, alas! It is easy for Islam to win over Christianity in Africa because the knowledge of the one God and the law it implies offer God to uncultivated minds without imposing a theology on them.

I pray never to see in this a sign of excellence and superiority. Yet I have always believed that the propagation of the Gospels is impeded at the start, not only with pagan peoples but in the capital too, because the short catechism, even in its most schematic form, demands from the child a conceptual knowledge of which he is incapable. And most remain incapable throughout their lives, like all primitive peoples. Everything should be focused on persuading children that Jesus, crucified under Pontius Pilate, rose from the dead and is still living, that all of His words have remained living, and that two have continued to be felt with an efficacy which these children can experience: the word which forgives sins, and the word which consecrates the breaking of bread.

The catechism should be concentrated on the teaching that God has revealed Himself to His creatures, that He was a child and a man like us, that He died and that His resurrection had many witnesses and they believed in Him, and that the living Christ never leaves us and that there are three essential forms of His presence: in the Living Bread we partake of at communion, but also in the state of grace if we have the joy of possessing it, because a soul in a state of grace manifests the spirit of God. The Lord Himself assures us of this: "My Father will love him and come to him and dwell within him." And finally, on each occasion when two or three come together to pray to the Lord, He has told us that He will be in our midst. A child convinced about these three modes of divine presence has no need to examine other mysteries until he grows older and wishes to know more. Beginning with the story of the Passion and going back to the Nativity, then retracing the way from the manger to the empty tomb, across Galilee and Judea, along the entire road the Lord took, in that concrete incarnate story which keeps close to the earth, the mysteries will come forth one after the other from the words and gestures of the Lord: the Trinity is therein announced and defined, as well as the primacy of Peter, and the Real Presence. No teaching should be given children in the form of doctrine but in the way by which it was revealed to the poor and the ignorant by the Lord Himself. The children in the catechism class can understand what the fishermen of the Sea of Tiberias understood.

VII

✵ ✵ ✵

The demon

❉ ❉ ❉

THE FACT IS that this light has been rejected. The fact is that men today refuse in advance, and without any preliminary examination, to believe the clue to the enigma is given to us outside of the material world. Modern man has cut off communication with God by a basic negation. He fears being surprised. The precaution of many writers today is to insure themselves against the risk of light, even at the last moment. The final unrepentance is carefully prepared by these brothers who have been as scrupulous in protecting themselves from God as we who love Him have been passionate in approaching Him and joining with Him.

We cannot accuse of inconsistency those who like Marxists believe only in the physical world. But this obsessive hate of Christianity which the surrealists feel is a mystery. They seek to surpass the real, to clear the way for an escape from the real world, and their means for this seem childish. They too tilt the magical device, but have recourse to obvious faking. They scorn and insult us who are sustained by the sacramental life as on a huge invisible peaceful river from birth to death, who live in a constant familiarity with the Spirit who conquered the world and who transcends time. Why do those insatiable surrealists, who are horrified by the world as it is today, hate us? Why do they curse the light, and with a hatred which logically cannot be felt for something that does not exist? Their hatred turns into an involuntary act of faith. They seem to be shouting: "You exist because I hate you. If you were not living, I would not try to kill you in the minds and the hearts of man."

This is what brings me to ask the question which so many Christians avoid and which I myself have always disliked facing. Do I believe in the spirit of evil? Do I believe there is someone? Haven't I at times taken refuge in the simple solution of imagining that it is a question of one symbol among many others which the Bible proposes to us? I prefer to avoid nothing about what I believe or do not believe concerning the existence of the demon and which must seem more unbelievable than anything else to agnostics and atheists.

On this point, as on so many others, I hold the two ends of the chain : an instinctive dislike to admit that a creature already so wretched and invulnerable has been released to an invisible enemy who has received the power to lead him into temptation, an enemy all the more to be feared because most men do not know he exists, or jokingly deny his existence. This is an excess of tribulation, as if it were important for someone to add to all the reasons for our being defeated a last irresistible reason. For what chance has a man over an angel who holds all the privileges of invisibility and ubiquity? A spirit, he reigns over spirits. He is the master of illusions and dreams, in a world which has announced God's death and which continues to exist outside of grace.

I agree it is in this respect that the problem of evil has disturbed me the most, and that I have often given over to the ease of the suggested compromises : the demon must be a symbol, an image-incarnation of the evil which is in us, the name given at the time of Jesus to all the illnesses which attack the spirit through the flesh. . . .

Now there is the opposite view. Throughout my

life I have had certainly not the proof but the impression that evil was truly and substantially someone. Men whom I knew to be great sinners gave me at no moment the impression that they might be possessed, whereas in others, whose lives seemed much less dissolute, I sensed a presence. Certain lives I have been able to observe over quite a long span of time have seemed to me diffused with a strange unclear light. This was doubtless only an impression. But a few confidential statements verify this. It is a fact that some people had to struggle all their lives against a presence they themselves did not hesitate to name.

I will refer to only one who spoke about this publicly and on many occasions: André Gide, whose example is all the more striking because at the end of his life there was no evidence that he could speak of the demon without laughing. Yet at certain periods he seems to have believed himself, if not possessed by the demon, at least to have had direct communication with him. In order to explain to agnostics the interest bordering on anguish which Gide's case inspired in his Christian friends, I quoted in *Mémoires Intérieurs* three texts (and I could have found many others of the same nature). The first two are from Gide himself. One is at the

beginning of the second part of *Si le grain ne meurt:*
"It has recently come to my attention that an important actor, the devil, might have taken part in
the drama. Nevertheless I will relate this drama
without first having intervene the one whom I will
identify much later." And here is the second text,
taken from the *Journal des Faux-Monnayeurs:* "On
certain days I feel such an invasion of evil that it
seems to me that already the prince of darkness is
setting about establishing in me a part of hell." The
last text I borrow from Julien Green, from a recent
page in which he describes Gide's behavior toward
him: "Since my return to France, in 1915, I have
not had an opportunity to see Gide without his trying, in some way or other, to weaken my faith."

How can we interpret the permission which, in
Holy Scripture, God gives the demon to "move over
the earth"? An angelic world exists whose real history is unknown to us and which it would be useless to try to penetrate. I believe that the life of the
sacraments protects us, certainly not from small or
serious defections, but that it holds off the enemy
about whom Gide also said (I quote from memory) :
"I do not believe in the demon, but that is what the
demon wishes: that I do not believe in him."

The devotion to the Virgin for the Catholic is in

one sense related to the certainty of an occult presence, of a prowler it is necessary to keep at a distance. I fear I will be accused of infantilism for
what I am writing here. . . . But how can I avoid
this? And what if truth indeed were childish? Rimbaud had the intuition that truth surrounds us with
its weeping angels. Perhaps Claudel was not in
error when, on that Christmas Sunday, he experienced the "eternal childhood of God." I have often
felt this myself, at Mass, as I watched a child coming back to his seat after communion. I am willing
that Christ be considered in proportion to the cosmos, but I easily lose interest in this concept. The
unbelievable truth I hold and which moves me is
that He lives in that child kneeling ahead of me,
the nape of whose thin neck I can see, and that He
is joined with him, allied with that offspring of man
in a resemblance which an adult has difficulty in
conceiving.

VIII

❋ ❋ ❋

The debt to Pascal

❋ ❋ ❋

ON THE OPENING page I stated that this book is
written for neither philosophers nor scholars. Not-
with standing this, Blaise Pascal is everywhere
present in it and I owe him this homage. Without
him, I doubt if I would have remained faithful, or
rather I have difficulty in imagining what, without
him, would have served as support for my faith at
periods of crisis in the history of my own life and
in the history of mankind. In a young man, the
hidden powers of the flesh and the demands of
reason are conjugated against Christ. In a large
measure, I owe to Pascal my resistance to this.

It is surprising that the writer to whom I owe
the most and who has influenced me the most, and
who was my master when I was sixteen, as soon as

I owned the *Pensées et Opuscules* in Braunschvig's edition, is still that today, and that the old man who turned journalist did not have to change schools, and in *Les Provinciales*, without ever finding it of course, looked for the secret of that lively wit which out of an ephemeral debate made an eternal debate.

But the strangest part of this story is that there is no other writer about whom I am less capable of speaking than about this Pascal to whom I owe everything, because one whole part of his genius eludes me, that aspect which, according to nature, defines him the best. That child geometrician, as soon as he was born to conscious life, belonged to science. We could imagine other points of meeting than those which gave Blaise Pascal over to Jansenist influences and which would have left him in a worldly situation. He would doubtless not have been less subtle than he was by nature. But the passion to convince would not have trained his mind, given over as it was to subtle problems, and would not have led him to the degree of perfection we see in the *Pensées*. On the other hand, no meeting is imaginable which would have made of him a mind indifferent to mathematics, to research and discovery.

The language of Pascal the mathematician and

geometrician is unfamiliar to me. I am the only one who never explored the ignorance separating me from him. This is what seems strange to me and this is what I must first confess: my incapacity to understand the research of a man who nevertheless has guided my life in this world, and perhaps in eternity. The man who, before his second conversion, had such an exalted feeling about the superiority of a mind like his own and about his domination over those who were inferior to him, turned away from science and came to us with ample proofs designed to impress and convince. Alone, these proofs would have collided in us with opposite proofs because so many different keys turn in the human lock. Moreover, we are suspicious that an apologist who wants to convince us at any cost has loaded the dice. But such a man brings us infinitely more than reasons. Blaise Pascal came to us and held in his hands a light, the lamp of those who are waiting for the return of the Bridegroom, a fire ignited by that flame he saw, with his own eyes, during the night of November 24, 1654, between approximately ten o'clock and twelve-thirty. It is that flame which still illuminates those of us who have kept faith in the God understood by the heart, because of Blaise Pascal and to a degree which God alone knows. I was twenty in those days when the Church of France was paying up for the Dreyfus case, when convents had been evacuated in the name of the law, when the encyclical *Pascendi* seemed to forbid a student like myself any contact with modern thought. I testify today that it was the Christ of Pascal who said to me, in those hours, "Stay with me."

This Jansenist, this defender of a doctrine under suspicion, this spirit free to the point of insolence and mockery within a Church unbending on matters of orthodoxy and within an absolute monarchy which had deified the state and imprisoned M. de Saint-Cyran, this rebel comes toward ignorant men like me with the light that was given him. And here we are on our knees beside him, and waiting for the inspiration of this humbled posture.

We knew what Christ had said to the saints, to Saint Teresa of Avila, to Saint John of the Cross; but we were not able to believe that what concerned those heroic souls could also concern us. Yet Pascal, despite his greatness, remains one of us. Like us, he was a reader of Montaigne. His prayers were those of a reader of Montaigne. He lived within the world's tumult, and spoke its language up until the end. *Le Mystère de Jésus* indicates the stages of the rapid mounting in the flaming night of a scientist, a man of letters, a polemicist and a journalist. It was to the satirist who will be revealed in *Les Provinciales*, to the proud passionate man whose very secret passions we do not know—who will ever know what they were?—it was to this brother that the Lord spoke the words which still inflame us who are the poor scribes of every age, whose profession is to dazzle and be praised by others. He speaks to each of us through Pascal. It is precisely for us, and in a language suitable for us, that He uttered words which one night I hesitated to say before a huge crowd because they rose up from the most intimate and most secret part of my being. "I thought of you in my suffering. Be consoled. You would not be looking for me if you had not found me. For you I have shed a drop of blood. Will you always have me shed the blood of my humanity without your shedding tears for me? I love you more fervently than you have loved your sins."

It is in the confidence of a friend speaking to his friend that we should study what these words, from generation to generation, have brought to those for whom they were said, and what they have given to me, and what they will continue to offer to the minds of a certain race of men, until the day which will perhaps come, which will surely come, when human memory will gradually lose its last treasures, when a last mesh of the net will be broken and *Le Mystère de Jésus* given back to the night. This evidence and this certainty is that Christ is in agony but that He is living. He does not agonize more in Russia or in China than in Italy and in France, but neither is He more alive here than there. All the reasons of the *Pensées* are as if inflamed by this certainty which preceded them.

Voltaire, in his *Remarques*, which (according to Sainte-Beuve) "seize upon Pascal alive under the hair shirt," was not wrong in contending with Pascal that it is not enough for a religion to take human nature into account in order to be true. Conformity between human nature and Christianity does not constitute a proof, and nothing can be concluded from this. But the fire, the burning flame which Pascal elevates over our heads and whose reflection illuminates his mask for all time, nothing could prevent from passing from one man to another, despite the free-thinkers of his age, and from passing through the century of the *Encyclopedia*, from being revived by the age of romanticism. Later, Zarathustra's *God is dead!* did not even cause it to flicker, although Nietzsche leveled attacks on

Pascal (whom he pitied as the noblest victim of Christ) which were more terrifying than Voltaire's. The negation of the modern world had no effect on those men for whom Pascal had come (and I am one of them).

It was necessary that once, only once, the revelation of the living Christ be given us by a man like ourselves—except for his genius—that it be given to the man of letters who had never bled under any hair shirt save that of his pride, and that he too should fall on his knees.

And if all the friends of Pascal have not known the joy, the tears of joy he shed that unforgettable night, at least all will have had some small or large part, each according to his capacity, in the peace he had promised them. The memory of those tears of joy and that peace is preserved on the paper Pascal carried sewn into his coat and of which there exists a copy from his own hand. Let us pause for a moment with this memorial, this parchment, this object, this thing there is no point in describing. A talisman, a charm: enough to make serious people shrug their shoulders. Paul Valéry denounced with an irritated pity this same Pascal "who wastes his time sewing bits of paper in his pockets at a moment when he should have given to France the glory of the calculus of infinity." I am one of those who are not scandalized by this parchment. It has come down to us through three centuries like the one signed by Faust—but a Christian Faust, and he signed it not with the spirit of darkness but with eternal love.

A talisman, a charm. It is strange to think that in the *avant-garde* of my generation, the descendants of Lautréamont and Rimbaud were bent upon escaping from reality by means of the subconscious and dreams, that drugs have maintained among us a tradition of suicide and madness—and we, in the literary rearguard, sons of Pascal, have held in our clasped hands a charm, not in order to escape reality but to reach supreme reality, not to change life but to change our own life, thanks to a continuous surpassing of ourselves.

And I could show, by confronting texts, that there is not much distance between that rearguard and that *avant-garde*, and that to certain flashes of Pascal answer from the opposite horizon flashes of Arthur Rimbaud.

Pascal is not a moralist trying to make us virtuous in the name of a rule created by a system. The Son of Man, who loves Pascal and whom Pascal loves, led him from the manger to the cross along roads which both knew. "I love Poverty because He loved it."

With a feeling of shame I grant that we will not find a similar parchment or talisman in the lining of the professorial coats of philosophers after Pascal. Moreover, almost all have refused Pascal the honor of being one of them. In their eyes he is not a philosopher, and neither is he a theologian for doctors in theology. I approve of this, and I admit they are right. He is not like philosophers and, according to Paul Valéry, he is the opposite of a philosopher. He was a man who believed that truth exists and is Someone. He claimed he knew truth and tried to persuade others, and did so not in an obscure language demanding an initiation but in an ordinary language an ordinary man can understand, the most precise and the purest language spoken in France, which never lost sight of the creature formed by nature and customs he wanted to convince. "He sees in a superior way what anyone can see!" Valéry says scornfully. Yes! but what if this were the sign of genius?

This is Pascal's scandal which arouses pity in professional philosophers. He provokes pity in them but he also shocks them. They consider his crime that of having tried to frighten us, of having taken pleasure

1 1 1

in prolonging our anguish to reach his ends. As if this anguish were not in each of us! Pascal does not create in us our troubled conscience, even if it is true he searches for its explanation and proposes to us its remedy. Wouldn't he himself have been more anxious than any of us? And why? He knew he was loved, and that one drop of blood had been shed for him. He possessed certainty, peace, joy and the "triumphant happiness of grace."

May there be in another century other men to bear homage to Pascal as we did one evening in 1962, solemnly, in the venerable Sorbonne. In those days to come, may there be another old man to rejoice over the answer that with Pascal, that thanks to Pascal, he will give to the question of Christ— the one He asked His disciples one day when almost all were leaving Him: "Do you too wish to leave me?" I alone can estimate what that edition of Léon Braunschvig of the *Pensées et Opuscules* meant for the faith of adolescents of my generation. May Blaise Pascal be thanked for all those who remained faithful. These believers did not trust solely in their instinctive feelings. They accepted a piece of evidence which comes from five words written on paper and sewn into the lining of a doublet: "Nobility of the human soul." And also nobility of the human mind. All material bodies together do not have the value of a single mind. All bodies and all minds together do not have the value of the slightest impulse of charity. Blaise Pascal went before us in this ascent from bodies to minds, and from minds to eternal Love.

You have only to look at him. If God does not exist, where does Blaise Pascal come from? Could blind inert matter have engendered that thought and language and insatiable heart? Nothing of what the Christian believes ever seemed to me more impossible than this madness you believe.

Pascal bears witness by the single fact that he exists. It is not even necessary any more that we open the edition of the *Pensées* of Braunschvig which had been given to us at school. In our closed fist we hold that invisible paper, that "Memorial" which we have never seen and yet which has not left us a single day during these past sixty years. Today we believe, as we believed at the beginning, that everything it states is true, that certainty exists, that peace on this earth can be reached, and joy. The fire of one night of Pascal was sufficient to illuminate our entire life, and like the child whom the night light reassures in his room full of shadows, because of that fire we are not afraid to go to sleep.

IX

❊ ❊ ❊

Prayer for faith

❁ ❁ ❁

"LORD, I BELIEVE. Come help my unbelief!" You
heard this prayer, Lord, with Your own ears when
You were a man, surrounded by other poor Gali-
leans. This small book of mine has expressed nothing save this contradiction. We believe in You
whom we do not see. We listen to Your words which
we do not hear. I say that You are in the wafer of
unleavened bread on my tongue. I meditate and
worship in me this presence of which nothing
perceptible gives proof. Several who were not
saints received signs: Claudel, Max Jacob, Simone
Weil. . . . Have I? If I claimed to have received
none during my life, I would lie. But if I told of
them, they would vanish as soon as I tried to put
them into words. And so many years cover over

those moments of grace that I am not sure of the memory I have of them. "Yes, I saw her! I saw her!" poor Bernadette repeated at her death. They had made her repeat so often in the convent parlor, for the edification of visitors, the story of the apparitions, that perhaps at the end she began to suspect she had dreamed them.

The two flashes—for it was as swift as a flash—whose burning I am trying to feel again occurred at the moment in my life which was the worst, I believe, and which is described on the pages of *Souffrances du chrétien.* For two or three years, it seemed as if I had lost my mind. Almost nothing of this was visible on the outside. The episodic reasons for this madness concealed more obscure reasons coming from the intersection of the flesh and the soul at that midway point in life when a man enters the forties. "When you think you are far from me," You said to the author of *The Imitation*, "it is often then that I am the closest!" I have often thought that You were never closer to me than those days of endless suffering when I could easily at any moment have plunged into death. I wandered about Paris like a lost dog, like a collarless dog. One day, worn out, I crossed the threshold of a chapel I had never seen, in a neighborhood which was not mine.

I entered this chapel for the first time and sat down
in the last row of chairs. I remember saying this
prayer to You. About that period we moved from
the rue de la Pompe to occupy another house. I
began going to the Benedictine chapel on the rue
de la Source. One weekday morning I had taken
communion and returned to my seat. My mind was
somewhat distracted. And suddenly I remembered
that day of suffering when I thought I had prayed
to You in vain. I could see the place where I had
sat down and the huge somber Christ I had prayed
to. It was as if Someone were saying to me: "Well,
don't you see?" O Lord, who do not belong to time,
You answered me in the hour of Your choice. What
I felt then that was unspeakable I cannot express or
even pretend to remember. I recall feeling joy and
love in the deepest recesses of my being. But I was
doubtless unworthy of this grace and it vanished, as
so many others did.

What else can I recall? One day, two or three
years earlier, because we were still living on the
rue de la Pompe, and it must have been the year of
Souffrances du chrétien, a short time after I had
regained peace, I was in the very small maid's room
we used to call the *cagibi* [nook], and where I used
to work, out of reach of my children. I am quite

sure it was the day of Pentecost. At least, it was the season of Pentecost. I don't remember whether I was reading, or working, or praying. Suddenly I fell on my knees, as if moved by some unknown force, overcome by some prodigious happiness. I wept and made no attempt to dry my tears. From that day on, Pentecost became my favorite feast day. If it had been my nerves and not the Spirit which brought me to my knees, how can one explain that never did I experience anything comparable, that never again did such an illumination overcome me, not a single time during the thirty-five years that followed, nor today when I am living, at least I hope I am, in an habitual state of grace. I could not report with assurance what this burning was exactly. In truth, I no longer remember it. And nothing else happened to me which might recall something about it.

I did not deserve to make one step farther in the direction of that joy which is bought at the price of a renunciation of all the sensual world. Of this I am not in the least capable. I acknowledge before You the degree to which I was the man who gives nothing, who gives up nothing, who has received the largest number of rewards in this world. I am crushed by these favors. This is not a means of evasion, or at least it does have a large degree of

sincerity. For You know that at certain moments
I uttered a cry of surprise and wonder, "Lord, why
didn't You abandon me?" Yes, why didn't You? At
that time I was a spoiled adolescent sensualist, forcing everything to comply to my satisfaction and
comfort, bent upon giving up nothing, neither the
world nor You, when only my egoism arrested my
coveteousness, when I took on lightheartedly the
responsibility and risks for others which the profession of a writer involves—when I arranged
everything, in order to win on all the rosters of eternity and time. O Lord, who do not like calculators
and unfaithful stewards, despite the difficult par-
able, or virtuous men, virtuous because they are
prudent and cowardly, something in me must have
disarmed You, since You did not abandon me—or
some saints interceded for me, someone who died
who had loved the young man I once was. But then,
we are judges of ourselves. What horrified me the
most about myself was perhaps what had the least
significance for You. The errors which humiliated
me the most were perhaps the first to be forgiven by
You. But You will ask me about what did not debase me or shame me or cause me to blush in the
least: namely, what perhaps kept You from return-
ing in the way You came to me once briefly on a

day of Pentecost in 1927 or 1928, in that small room. . . . Claudel wrote: "Allow me to find once again the source of those forgotten tears." Those tears which I was never again worthy of shedding before You.

But again, isn't it my joy I miss? The doorway which the saints went through I have never even approached. I have remained a stranger to the passion, to Your passion. The sign I make with my hand on my body, and which is above the bed where I sleep and on the table where I work, has been stripped by me of its meaning. I am irritated if someone speaks to me about "the consolations of religion" and yet what else have I done all my life save look for them? And more than ever at this final moment in my life, what else have I done except try to recover a certain gentleness, a certain tenderness which once I had known when I was a schoolboy who enjoyed weeping at first-communion Masses? Lord, I do not believe that You rejected me because of my incurable hedonism, but I believe that it impeded and immobilized me at the beginning of my life and that I did not take one more step toward You, even at the time of great quiet and peace, whereas my old age is sanctified, in spite of me, by my communion on the Living Bread. I did

not understand that the first signs You gave me
were signs to free me and allow me to move toward
You. I have remained motionless, bound by my
habits of a sensualist, waiting to be consoled once
again. And of course I was consoled at the spot
where I stayed. I did not take the road leading to
contemplation and possession and therefore to certainty. I sat down on a milestone resigned to going
no farther, encumbered with countless useless ob-
jects, with all the luggage I drag after me.

Lord, am I not finding satisfaction even in this
avowal? Am I not looking for pleasure under Your
gaze as I try to cleanse myself? Am I not a simulator
at this very moment as I write these lines? This
image of myself which I am sketching under Your
gaze and which claims to be overpowering in reality
I take pleasure in, and as it is formed by these
words, I doubt if it offers many points in common
with the being I really am and whose exact measurement only You can take.

Whether we debase ourselves or elevate ourselves
in Your presence, whether we recite the prayer of
the Publican or of the Pharisee, I fear there is always in it an insincere attitude, a deliberate manner
of behavior, of a character whose actions we imagine
please You, when we are only playacting before

You. That character joins the one the public demands we be, and to whom we adjust instinctively, to the extent of really becoming the character.

Lord, now in Your presence I have reached the last proof of faith: it cannot be weighed and judged with certainty. It is impossible to remove from it all the suspect elements, especially in a writer whose profession is fiction, pretense and lies. Tartuffe's imposture is less simple than Molière believed. His impostor is a scoundrel of the most commonplace type, who seizes upon an imbecile the like of whom there aren't many and exploits him. But we who are not scoundrels, who are not trying to trick an imbecile, are trying to make You our dupe. It is because of some idea concerning ourselves which we create out of our existence that we speak with the words of the Christian which we are not. We have been crucified only in spite of ourselves and we have desired nothing more than not to be crucified.

The world does not in the least need to tell us to come down from our cross! Lord, our lies, our disguise, our imposture are so evident, so flagrant, that there is no point in questioning them. What remains a question is what You alone know and see. If there exists at the very heart of the lie an atom of truth and sincerity—"If you have faith, though it be but like a grain of mustard seed, you have only to say to this mountain . . ."—I cannot doubt Your grace in me. This atom, therefore, no matter how tiny it is, exists and sends out its rays.

This is the final retreat in which *what I believe* is concentrated, and which is the subject of this book. "For if our heart condemn us, God is greater than our heart." I have meditated on this sentence from the First Epistle of Saint John and quoted it countless times. One day this sentence returned to my mind as if it had been rewritten by Your own hand for my personal use. This happened under conditions I have related several times. I have often told the story of the prayer book which Colette had asked me for. I would not dream of placing this strange incident among the signs You have given me, if there were not a connection with the sentence of Saint John. Let me, then, briefly, relate this story. During the course of a luncheon at the darkest moment of the Occupation, Colette asked me pointblank for a missal, but asked me not to buy her one. She described the one she wanted, which, she claimed, I would find somewhere in my own house: one of those old prayer books of an earlier generation, bound in black sheepskin "which are kept in families." I promised her I would look for it. I did look, but found nothing.

Three days later I received a strange letter from her. She told me that her concierge had handed to her the prayer book she had described to me. But it had not come from me, as she had first believed. It was a Polish friend who was in a Paris hospital for a fatal operation and who had sent her this final remembrance. Colette telephoned her, and after thanking her, asked: "But why this prayer book?" The foreign friend hesitated and answered: "You will think I am mad, but you came to me in a dream and asked me for the prayer book. . . ." Colette urged me to come and see for myself. Immediately I went to the rue de Montpensier. It was exactly the black prayer book she had described to me. As I examined it carefully, Colette told me that the foreign lady had written a few words on the first page. I could hardly believe what I read, for it was the sentence of Saint John: "For if our heart condemn us, God is greater than our heart." I knew that this part of the message concerned me. And still today I know the answer to the question asked in the title of this book: *What I Believe*. I believe I am loved such as I was, such as I am, such as my own heart sees me, judges me and condemns me. It is hard to convince oneself of this, and this is true for each believer in particular. "Greatness of the human soul." However mediocre and corrupt and stupid we are, there is a point in each of us where You are attached, and it is this divine attachment which moves Your compassion for us. It is the tenderness of God, both Son of God and Son of Man. There would be no idiots and no bores for us if we could see far enough into this part of them, the part which You know and where You are, if it is a soul in a state of grace where You reside. (At the moment of correcting this page, a doubt comes to me. I wonder if the sentence of Saint John had not been written on the first page of a pious tract which Colette received about the same time, from a poor girl she had never seen, who suffered for her. Colette knew about this.)

I am a writer, Lord, and You are the subject of my book, and I will pay dearly for having written it. "The writer, the murderer and the prostitute . . ." that terrible abridgment of Paul Claudel is branded on the deepest part of my being. But from his childhood on, You have shown Your love for this writer. You entered his heart on the morning of May 12, 1896, when angelic voices were singing *Tabernacle redoutable* and *Le Ciel a visité la Terre.* . . . Now

I see clearly that You never once thought of abandoning me, no matter what I did. I see that every judgment is rash, and the judgment we make about ourselves is no less rash than that of others. We do not know ourselves. We seem to take it upon ourselves to discourage Your justice ahead of time. There is no impulse in us which is not ambiguous, which does not conceal a dark calculation, no gesture which does not come from a pose we believe we profit from, a pose we take in Your presence or in the presence of our own conscience, or in the presence of other men.

What is left in me of which I can take advantage? Nothing, in the texture of infidelity which constitutes a long life, save that thread which starts at the beginning and which has never been broken. All the rest of the material is in shreds. The thread You hold remains, and to it is attached the heart whose beats no one in the world counts any longer, this heart which is a petrification of old sins, a dead weight of sediment : what the tide leaves on the sand, the foam of an endless youth—what is forgiven but which cannot not have taken place. We are sculptured forever : no one of our traits can be destroyed in the future.

I believe I am forgiven. It is not the easiest to

believe in from among all the things I have believed in. And yet that is the one about which I should be the most convinced, since I am now at the moment of my decline and have assumed the habits which were my mother's when she had reached the age I am today. I am once again at the same Mass she attended in the black dawn of winter or in the light of a summer morning. I am once again overcome with the same silence that should be enough to free us from all worry and give over our past life to that mercy living in us and which is You, O Bread of Life!

Yet I give over to one last scruple: What we call inner life, life with You, joins that turning in on oneself, that maniacal constant attention which the writer concentrates on his own person, the one subject matter of his work. The demands of salvation become the disguise for that cult of the self which a writer taught me when I was twenty, and which ennobles with too fine a pretext my indifference to others.

I do not see clearly whether it is grace which uses the worst in us for its own purposes or whether it is our demon who turns aside for his own profit the action of grace in us. It was perhaps at the center of this contradiction that our destiny took shape, and that our face with its irregular and contrasting features was forever fixed. That is why I ask You for this last favor, Lord: that my life with You will at last enter into contact with my brothers and be felt by them, but not with an intent to attack and crush them. It is unbelievable and yet true that my life has nurtured the joyous combativeness of a polemicist who nails down his enemy, and does not try to win him over and convince him, but to come out ahead of him. Lord, I ask You for this last miracle, to allow me, in spite of myself, to enter upon charity, since I am incapable of reaching it myself, since the gifts I have received from You, and the vocation I have believed to be mine, commit me to a debate which too often degenerates into a dispute, and since everything in the writer irresistibly turns into the desire to shine and dominate.

You, whose heart is gentle and humble, teach me that gentleness and humility I am certainly capable of conceiving. I have loved gentleness in men. I have expected it and even demanded it of them, and I have almost never encountered it. . . . And yet how pitiless I have been myself! In You, this contradiction in my nature is resolved. In You I have rediscovered the source of a gentleness I loved as a child and lost.

Finally I ask from You the strength and the courage to remain in Your presence, not to move away when You are here, not to escape into dreams, into vain fantasies, as is my custom. Everything is an excuse, even for those of us who pretend to love You, not to stay with You. We are like those Jews who were afraid of dying and who withdrew from before Your face. Lord, allow me to meditate in the peace of Your presence, so that when my hour comes, I will pass without any sense of transition from You to You, from You as Living Bread, the Bread of men, to You as Love already possessed by those among my beloved ones who went to sleep before me in Your love.

Amen.

X

❀ ❀ ❀

Repentance

✹ ✹ ✹

I REFUSE TO delete anything from this book, but on rereading it, I feel scruples about two points. First, some of my words show coldness for the visible Church, or at least deliberate indifference and detachment with regard to its organization and its entire human structure.

I understand it better, at the moment of writing this, at the time when in Rome the Ecumenical Council has just begun, and when Pope John XXIII has spoken the words of mercy I always wanted to hear in Rome. He said them in the presence of our separated brothers and at this high point of glory he was able to efface himself and blot out his own personality, in such a way that through this old man the Holy Spirit itself, the Spirit of love and consolation, spoke to the world. Yes, at last I understand the strength of my devotion to Holy Church, even in its aspect of a human society and despite the relationship in the past between its history and that of Caesar.

I was certainly one of her respectful sons. But that majestic inflexible Mother did not seem to know of my desires and aspirations. Barely had I articulated them when I was blamed. Between the encyclical *Pascendi* and the condemnation of *Le Sillon*, in the early days of my youth, and the condemnation of the worker-priests at the end of my life, the massive inevitable Roman bureaucracy, without scandalizing me, because I knew it was necessary, had finally persuaded me that all I hoped for and expected from the Church would always be impeded, that indefinitely I would see the saints kindle again a small flame which had been put out after being ignited. Should I express my complete thought? Under the last pontificate, which was so brilliant in appearance, the radiant person of the Sovereign Pontiff seemed to me, rightly or wrongly, not to correct anything and to aggravate everything.

For the first time since my youth, the Holy Spirit has been made manifest visibly, at least to me. The one force which can win over the most powerful obstacles resides today in Rome. Peter is no longer that old man isolated and even imprisoned by his servants. I see him surrounded by all his sons, and even by those who had asked for their part of the inheritance and who had withdrawn from him. And now he pronounces no anathema, no curse, and all nations turn toward the prow of the ancient boat, more impressed by the sight of the fisher of men than they were, during the course of this year 1962, by the explorers of the cosmos.

What I believe, what I have always believed, I see and touch at last: the Gospel has preserved this power over the hearts of men whose Christian nations, obsessed by the spirit of conquest, have misused and abused for a thousand years, and it remains intact, and humanity will never renounce this hope.

Thus the sixth Pope to whom I have been obedient (I was born during the pontificate of Leo XIII), the humblest of all, has scattered the cloud of distrust, the vague resentment in which I lived, with regard to Rome, except at the time of Pius XI.

One other part of this small book troubles me: the impression I may give to readers of the preceding chapter. They might believe that I received tangible signs and that it is important to receive signs. However, what I have reported may have been illusory. In reality, it is of little importance, and even of no importance at all. I would be deceiving those who are hesitating in crossing the threshold to lead them to believe that a sign will be given them. To have faith is to believe what one doesn't see, to love what one doesn't feel, because what one feels belongs to nature, comes from nature, and therefore depends upon flesh and blood. If it is God who consoles us, or if it is we speaking to ourselves, it is not incumbent on us to clear up the matter—especially an old writer, a professional fable-maker who knows that he must be wary, more than other men, of the power he has of inventing creatures and speech, and that between his own fervor and the dryness which a soul complains of in confiding to him, there is perhaps only the distance separating an author from someone who is not an author.

You then who have heard the call of the Lord and have decided to answer it, you will perhaps enter upon darkness and silence, or even upon fatigue and disgust—and this will have no more significance than the joy with which you will overflow. On every page of the Gospel, the Lord asks for faith. "Men of little faith," He said with grief as He looked at His followers. But He was deeply moved by the woman from Canaan and the centurion. Their faith was the same as their love. The old pilgrim I am, about to reach the goal of my pilgrimage, sets up his tent for the last time in the heart of the country circumscribed by the words "You exist because of my love . . ." To believe is to love.